PERSONAL THEMES IN LITERATURE

THE MULTICULTURAL EXPERIENCE

◀ **Sally Jorgensen, Ph. D.** ▶
Valerie Whiteson, Ph. D.

If we do not honor our past,
we lose our future.
If we destroy our roots,
we cannot grow.

Friedensreich Hundertwasser

PRENTICE HALL REGENTS
Englewood Cliffs, New Jersey 07632

Personal themes in literature: the multicultural experience/
  [compiled by] Sally Jorgensen, Valerie Whiteson.
    p. cm.
  ISBN 0-13-013418-X
  1. Readers—Social sciences. 2. Pluralism (Social sciences)—
  Problems, exercises, etc. 3. English language—Textbooks for
  foreign speakers. 4. Ethnic relations—Problems, exercises, etc.
  I. Jorgensen, Sally. II. Whiteson, Valerie Lily.
  PE1127.S6P46 1993
  428.6'4—dc20

                                                            92–45100
                                                            CIP

Acquisitions editor: *Nancy Leonhardt*
Managing editor: *Sylvia Moore*
Editorial/production supervision
  and interior design: *Christine McLaughlin Mann*
Electronic art: *Freddy Flake*
Cover illustration: *Anna Price–Oneglia*
Cover design: *Yes Graphics*
Interior illustrations: *Ann Elizabeth Thiermann*
Copyeditor: *Sandra Di Somma*
Pre-press buyer: *Ray Keating*
Manufacturing buyer: *Lori Bulwin*

©1993 by Prentice Hall Regents
Prentice-Hall, Inc.
A Paramount Communications Company
Englewood Cliffs, New Jersey 07632

Every attempt has been made to obtain permission to print "Who Am I" by Tru Vu, and
excerpts from *The Nowhere Man* by Kamala Markandaya. This book may not be sold or
distributed in the state of Israel.

Printed in the United States of America

10   9   8   7   6   5   4   3

ISBN   0-13-013418-X

Prentice-Hall International (UK) Limited, *London*
Prentice-Hall of Australia Pty. Limited, *Sydney*
Prentice-Hall Canada Inc., *Toronto*
Prentice-Hall Hispanoamericana, S.A., *Mexico*
Prentice-Hall of India Private Limited, *New Delhi*
Prentice-Hall of Japan, Inc., *Tokyo*
Simon & Schuster Asia Pte. Ltd., *Singapore*
Editora Prentice-Hall do Brasil, Ltda., *Rio de Janeiro*

CONTENTS

INTRODUCTION TO THE TEACHER   v
INTRODUCTION TO THE STUDENT   viii
ACKNOWLEDGEMENTS   x

▼ UNIT 1: IDENTITY ▼   1
Section

1 "My Name" by Sandra Cisneros   2
Writing Strategy Lesson: Making Comparisons with
                        Metaphors and Similes   4
2 "Boys and Girls" by Sandra Cisneros   5
3 "No One Else" by Elaine Laron   9
4 "Girl" by Jamaica Kincaid   11
5 "Who Am I?" by Tru Vu   16
6 "A House of My Own" by Sandra Cisneros   19

▼ UNIT 2: MEMORIES ▼   21
Section

1 "Goldfields Hotel" by Valerie Whiteson   22
Writing Strategy Lesson: Descriptive Language   27
2 "Boricua" by Tato Laviera   29
3 "A Day's Wait" by Ernest Hemingway   33
4 "Chinatown Talking Story" by Kitty Tsui   40
5 "The Jacket" by Gary Soto   48

▼ UNIT 3: RELATIONSHIPS ▼   56
Section

1 "Seaman's Ditty" by Gary Snyder   57
2 "A Choice of Weapons" by Phyllis McGinley   60
3 Excerpts from "Four Directions" and "Double Face" from
   The Joy Luck Club by Amy Tan   62
Writing Strategy Lesson: Point of View   70

4A "What Sally Said" by Sandra Cisneros **72**

4B "Linoleum Roses" by Sandra Cisneros **75**

▼ UNIT 4: CHANGES ▼ 79

Section

1 Verse from "Ecclesiastes" **80**

Writing Strategy Lesson: Transitional Techniques **83**

2 Excerpt from *The Nowhere Man* by Kamala Markandaya **84**

3 Excerpt from *The Rain Child* by Margaret Laurence **92**

4 "Okasan/Mother" by Sakae S. Roberson **100**

5 Excerpt from *Act One* by Moss Hart **106**

6 "Obstacle" by Sally Jorgensen **116**

▼ UNIT 5: WORKING 119

Section

1 "To Be of Use" by Marge Piercy **120**

2 "The First Job" by Sandra Cisneros **124**

Writing Strategy Lesson: Tone of Voice **128**

3 Excerpt from *I Know Why the Caged Bird Sings* by Maya Angelou **130**

4 "Señor Payroll" by William Barrett **140**

INTRODUCTION TO THE TEACHER

The choice of reading selections in *Personal Themes in Literature: The Multicultural Experience* is driven by three overriding convictions: (1) that good literature can model and inspire language learning; (2) that readings should reflect diverse cultural perspectives and experiences; and (3) that a strong personal voice should come through in the readings to enhance students' identification with and understanding of the material. The selections are relatively short and include poetry, short stories, and excerpts from novels. We have sought to find material that is psychologically sophisticated, intellectually stimulating, highly engaging, and yet also *linguistically accessible*. The illustrations throughout the book are also intended to enhance the readings and broaden the ways that meaning is conveyed—through visual, not just verbal means.

We have chosen respected international authors, some of whom are newer, emerging authors. A personal voice comes through in the readings that honestly and authentically conveys individual perceptions and experiences. One consequence of this orientation is that some of the selections may be considered controversial. For example, several selections deal with ethnic discrimination, particularly "Goldfields Hotel," the excerpt from Maya Angelou's *I Know Why the Caged Bird Sings*, and "Señor Payroll." Cisneros's short stories, "What Sally Said" and "Linoleum Roses," look at child abuse and wife abuse. "The First Job" touches upon the issue of sexual harassment. We believe these issues to be relevant and important to students and to their survival in the world today. You may omit readings if you choose. Although the units and sections within units are meaningfully sequenced, the book is not rigidly structured and can be adapted to the needs of different instructional situations.

We also believe that "the general is found in the particular" and that universal themes can be derived from these individualistic writings. The units themselves are organized around themes that represent major facets of our life experiences: Identity, Memories, Relationships, Changes, and Working. The five units are in turn divided into sections. Each section contains reading selections that are preceded by "prereading exercises." These exercises provide a schema or framework for the passage and provoke students' thinking about a particular idea or issue. They can take the form of a brief writing activity or a class discussion, in accordance with time constraints and teacher preferences.

The reading selection is then presented, along with an introduction to the author. It is followed by (1) Vocabulary Exercises (as needed), (2) Comprehension Questions or Comprehension Exercises; and (3) Topics for Discussion or Writing. Each unit also contains a Writing Strategy Lesson. Vocabulary activities are provided so students can practice using some of the more difficult words in particular reading passages. These have been kept to a minimum since it is preferable that you design exercises tailored to the vocabulary needs of your class. The format of comprehension exercises is varied to maintain interest and diversify the ways that students manifest their understanding of the material. These exercises and questions serve as a "comprehension check" and require literal, objective recounting and analysis of the reading selection. They ask for text-centered responses, not personal opinion. Student answers can and should be framed in their own words, however. (Because there is often a range of acceptable ways to phrase responses to the comprehension questions, providing a teacher's manual with "right answers" did not seem to us to be appropriate or necessary for this text.)

Following the comprehension exercises are topics for discussion and writing, which shift the focus to more subjective, reader-centered responses. Higher level generalizations are solicited, as well as personal associations and interpretations of the material. Several different topics are suggested in order to provide variety and flexibility for you and for students. The topics represent varying levels of complexity and sophistication and lend themselves to different instructional strategies. Some topics can be used to trigger conversation practice, such as through collaborative, in-class activities or out-of-class interviews. Some lend themselves to brief writing exercises; others to longer, more in-depth writing assignments. The topics can also be adapted to different writing forms: students may choose to keep a private journal, write a poem, or develop a more formal essay. (One approach for longer assignments is to have students go back through the topics in all of the sections after they have completed a unit and choose one topic to write about.) Special effort has been made to suggest fresh and imaginative topics to stimulate students' curiosity and creativity and to tap into their personal experiences in ways they may not have thought of before. Oral and written communication activities should draw from things students know and care about.

Included in each unit is a Writing Strategy Lesson. Frequently, too, there are follow-up exercises in subsequent units. The topics of these lessons are as follows:

▼ Unit 1: Making comparisons with metaphors and similes
▼ Unit 2: Descriptive language
▼ Unit 3: Point of view
▼ Unit 4: Transitional techniques
▼ Unit 5: Tone of voice

The reason for including these lessons is to make the writing styles of the selected authors more *apparent*—to have students notice some of the techniques and literary devices that writers use to make their writing more effective, more expressive. We want to help students be cognizant of why certain passages are especially vivid, interesting, moving, or funny. Students are asked to identify particular writing strategies in the passages they have just read, to practice them in short exercises, then to try to incorporate them in their own writing assignments. The purpose is not so much for students to memorize literary terms, as it is to help them internalize different approaches and expand their repertoire of effective writing techniques.

Language learning is inherently interesting and purposeful for the infant. Both the content and context of communication are relevant to their experience. The psychologist B. F. Skinner has written that babies' babblings are pleasurable and self-reinforcing for them. Their own voice is their best teacher. We have tried to transfer these principles to adolescents' and adults' development of higher level skills in their native language or their learning of English as a foreign language. Both processes should be inherently interesting, relevant, purposeful, pleasurable, and self-reinforcing. Students' own voices are their best teacher. We hope we have succeeded. We also hope that *you* enjoy using the book and welcome your reactions and suggestions.

Sally Jorgensen, Ph.D.
Educational Consultant
Santa Cruz, California

Valerie Whiteson, Ph.D.
Faculty Member
Evergreen Valley College
San Jose, California

INTRODUCTION TO THE STUDENT

This is not an ordinary textbook. Students who have used it tell us that they take it to bed to read, as though it were a private journal or a novel they can't put down. The readings touch their own experiences and have meaning for them. What comes through in the stories and poems is a personal voice, revealing life experiences in an honest and engaging way. These experiences might be an anxious first day on a new job; the sad, sweet memory of a first love; or the strangeness of living in a new land, uprooted from familiar places and familiar routines.

Personal Themes in Literature: The Multicultural Experience contains reading selections and activities to help you improve your understanding and mastery of English. It is divided into five units, each dealing with an important facet of life: Identity, Memories, Relationships, Changes, and Working. The first unit, Identity, explores how you see yourself, how you think others see you, and what they expect of you. It also asks you to look into your future: What do you see for yourself?

Unit 2 looks back at childhood memories. Did you like yourself as a child? What is your favorite childhood memory? Are you a better parent than your parents were to you?

Unit 3 deals with relationships in all the different forms they can take—romantic relationships, parent-child relationships, friendships. Relationships are often perceived differently by the two people involved. The "story" of a relationship would be told differently depending upon who's telling it.

Unit 4 explores major life changes that come about sometimes by our own doing and sometimes because of forces outside of ourselves. People respond differently to physical, cultural, and financial changes that shake up their lives. Why do some people feel comfortable in a new culture and others cling to the past? What changes have you gone through in your own life?

Unit 5 looks at our work life. Much of our life is spent in the workplace, and what we do and who we are there guide many other options and choices. Doing a job well and feeling competent are a source of great pleasure and pride. Work that we don't enjoy or feel good about can cause frustration and stress. Is there an accomplishment that you are especially proud of? Were you recognized for it?

It is our belief that the best way to learn a new language or improve one's writing ability is to be exposed to people who use language well. Listen to the voice that comes through in the reading selections. Look at the ways the authors express emotion, convey ideas, and paint pictures with words. Then think about your own experience. Write about what you know and feel. Struggle to find the perfect words to express things that you may never have put into words before. Find your own voice. Come away from this book not only with a greater command of English, but also with an appreciation for the uniqueness of your own life and confidence in your own truths.

ACKNOWLEDGEMENTS

We especially want to acknowledge the authors of the readings we have chosen for the book. We thank them for their wonderful words. Thanks also to two artists from Santa Cruz, California, for enhancing these words with evocative and skillfully rendered artwork: Anna Price–Oneglia for the cover painting and Ann Elizabeth Thiermann for the illustrations. We wish to thank, too, the teachers at both college and high school levels around the country who reviewed the materials and field tested them with their students. Their suggestions were enormously helpful in revising and improving the book. It has been important to us to prepare a textbook that is instructionally sound, as well as enjoyable for students *and* teachers.

Personal Themes in Literature: The Multicultural Experience evolved from a 1988 text, co-authored by Valerie Whiteson-Klasewitz, Ph.D. and Nava Horovitz, entitled *Themes in Prose and Poetry: Focus on Vocabulary*, published by University Publishing Projects, Ltd., in Israel. We appreciate their generosity in allowing us to draw from the material in that book. During our initial research to diversify the cultural representation in the reading selections, one person who pointed us in some new and fruitful directions was Richard E. Sherwin, a faculty member at Bar Ilan University in Tel Aviv. At the time, Dick was teaching English at the University of California at Santa Cruz.

Special thanks to our editors at Prentice Hall—Anne Riddick, our first editor, and Nancy Leonhardt, who guided the book through to the end. We enjoyed working with the Production Editor, Christine McLaughlin Mann, and Cover Designer, Marianne Frasco. Their enthusiasm and creative ideas re–energized us at the end of a long process! We appreciate, too, Nancy's Assistant, Terry TenBarge, for her efficient and responsive communications.

Sally Jorgensen
Valerie Whiteson

UNIT 1 IDENTITY

The theme of this unit is IDENTITY. Our identity is who we are—separate and unique from everyone else. It takes shape as our lives unfold. Our experiences and relationships can reflect different aspects of ourselves. Our identity (also referred to as our "self-concept") could be thought of as a fabric that weaves together threads from past experiences, inherited tendencies, feelings, thoughts, and actions. The choices we make in life and our hopes and dreams for the future arise from this fabric that is our personality. This unit asks you to explore your own identity and the threads that make up the unique fabric that is you.

Some of the topics for discussion and writing may be ones that you would like to include in a personal notebook of your own writings and poems. You may also include pictures or photographs with these entries, or make drawings to go with them.

SECTION 1

PREREADING

Before you read this passage, think about your own name. How do you feel about your name? Do you like it or not? Take a few minutes and write about your feelings. You may want to share your ideas with a classmate, your teacher, or the whole class. If you prefer, write your answer in your private journal.

The first two readings are from Sandra Cisneros's book *The House on Mango Street*. In each of the stories, the narrator explores her identity—who she is—by comparing and contrasting herself to others.

MY NAME
Sandra Cisneros

In English my name means hope. In Spanish it means too many letters. It means sadness, it means waiting. It is like the number nine. A muddy color. It is the Mexican records my father plays on Sunday mornings when he is shaving, songs
5 like sobbing.

It was my great-grandmother's name and now it is mine. She was a horse woman too, born like me in the Chinese year of the horse—which is supposed to be bad luck if you're born female—but I think this is a Chinese lie because the Chinese, like the
10 Mexicans, don't like their women strong.

My great-grandmother. I would've liked to have known her, a wild horse of a woman, so wild she wouldn't marry until my great-grandfather threw a sack over her head and carried her off. Just like that, as if she were a fancy chandelier. That's the
15 way he did it.

And the story goes she never forgave him. She looked out the window all her life, the way so many women sit their sadness on an elbow. I wonder if she made the best with what she got or was she sorry because she couldn't be all the things she
20 wanted to be. Esperanza. I have inherited her name, but I don't want to inherit her place by the window.

At school they say my name funny as if the syllables were made out of tin and hurt the roof of your mouth. But in Spanish my name is made out of a softer something, like silver, not quite
25 as thick as sister's name Magdalena which is uglier than mine. Magdalena who at least can come home and become Nenny. But I am always Esperanza.

I would like to baptize myself under a new name, a name more like the real me, the one nobody sees. Esperanza as
30 Lisandra or Maritza or Zeze the X. Yes. Something like Zeze the X will do.

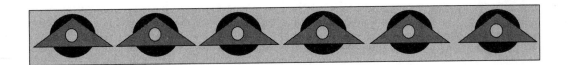

COMPREHENSION EXERCISE

Complete the sentences with the correct information from the story.

1. The name of the person narrating the story is _____.

2. She is named after _____.

3. In English her name means _____.

4. In Spanish her name means _____.

5. Both she and her great-grandmother are called "horse woman"

   because _____.

6. She would like to baptize herself under a new name, such as

   _____.

COMPREHENSION QUESTIONS

1. Why doesn't the narrator like her name?

2. What does she know about her great-grandmother's life, and what does she wonder about it?

TOPICS FOR DISCUSSION OR WRITING

1. What does your name mean in your culture? Were you named after anyone? Do you have a nickname? If so, how did you get it?
2. If you could change your name, what would you change it to and why?
3. Interview one or two other people about their names. Ask if they like their names. Also ask them questions 1 and 2.

WRITING STRATEGY LESSON: MAKING COMPARISONS WITH METAPHORS AND SIMILES

Good writers often use *metaphors* and *similes*, which are comparisons between two unlike things, in order to enrich their descriptions of a person, place, or experience. These are not *literal* comparisons, but more abstract, imaginative, *figurative* comparisons between things not usually thought of as similar. For example, at the end of the third paragraph in the story "My Name," the narrator says that her great-grandfather threw a sack over her great-grandmother's head and carried her away as though she were a "fancy chandelier." How does this comparison of her body to a fancy chandelier help you better understand how her great-grandfather felt about his bride-to-be?

The author has used a simile (pronounced SI'-MI-LEE) because the word *as* precedes the comparison. A *metaphor* is also a comparison between unlike things, but the signal words *like* or *as* are not present to alert the reader to the upcoming comparison. The narrator uses a metaphor when she says her great-grandmother was "a wild horse of a woman."

Now it's your turn. Think up metaphors or similes for the following sentences. Be original in your descriptions. Don't simply give the most common response.

1. The clouds are a/an _____

_____.

2. The baby's skin was soft as _____

_____.

3. My boss was so angry that she became a/an _____

_____.

4. The cake tasted like _____

_____.

Which of the four sentences are metaphors and which are similes?

SECTION 2

PREREADING

Write five sentences about yourself. Make some of them true and others false. Pair up with a classmate and have this person try to guess which of the statements about you are true and which are false.

In the next selection from Sandra Cisneros's *The House on Mango Street*, entitled "Boys and Girls," the narrator thinks about herself in relation to her friends. In the passage she compares herself to a particular object in order to describe how she sees herself. Can you identity the metaphor in the next story?

BOYS AND GIRLS
Sandra Cisneros

The boys and girls live in separate worlds. The boys in their universe and we in ours. My brothers for example. They've got plenty to say to me and Nenny inside the house. But outside they can't be seen talking to girls. Carlos and Kiki are each
5   other's best friend . . . not ours.
Nenny is too young to be my friend. She's just my sister and that was not my fault. You don't pick your sisters, you just get them and sometimes they come like Nenny.
She can't play with those Vargas kids or she'll turn out just like
10   them. And since she comes right after me, she is my responsibility.

Some day I will have a best friend all my own. One I can tell my secrets to. One who will understand my jokes without my having to explain them. Until then I am a red balloon, a
15 balloon tied to an anchor.

COMPREHENSION EXERCISE

Are these statements true or false? Circle the right answer. If the answer is not correct, revise it so that it reads correctly.

TRUE   FALSE   **1.** Nenny is the narrator's best friend.

TRUE   FALSE   **2.** The narrator's brothers talk to her when they are in the house, but not when they are outside because she is a girl.

TRUE   FALSE   **3.** Nenny is older than the narrator.

TRUE   FALSE   **4.** According to the story, it's important to have a best friend to tell your secrets to.

WRITING STRATEGY ACTIVITIES

1. What is the metaphor in the story? What does it tell you about how the speaker sees herself?
2. What makes it a metaphor and not a simile? Rewrite the sentence in the story that contains the metaphor so that the description is a simile.

TOPICS FOR DISCUSSION OR WRITING

1. The narrator uses the metaphor "a red balloon tied to an anchor" to describe herself. Think of a metaphor to describe yourself—an object or image that reveals something important about you. Write about it, and also draw or find a picture of your "self-concept" metaphor.
2. Throughout your life, who would you say has been your best friend? Describe your relationship and what made it special. What did your friend see in you that you especially liked?

SECTION 3

PREREADING

Write for a few minutes about something you do especially well and something you don't do well. You may want to share your ideas with a classmate, your teacher, or the whole class. If you prefer, write your answer in your private journal.

Although we are taught many things in our lives and are often told how we should think and feel about things, our thoughts and feelings are still our own. They are part of the fabric of our identity that makes us unique and different from others. The following poem by Elaine Laron defends these "rights" to be ourselves.

NO ONE ELSE
Elaine Laron

People can tell you how
To multiply by three
And someone else can tell you how
To spell Schenectady
5 And someone else can tell you how
To ride a two-wheeled bike
But no one else, no, no one else
Can tell you what to like.

An engineer can tell you how
10 To run a railroad train
A map can tell you where to find
The capital of Spain
A book can tell you all the names
Of every star above
15 But no one else, no, no one else
Can tell you who to love.

Your aunt Louise can tell you how
To plant a pumpkin seed
Your cousin Frank can tell you how
20 To catch a centipede
Your mom and dad can tell you how
To brush between each meal
But no one else, no, no one else
Can tell you how to feel.

25 For how you feel is how you feel
And all the whole world through
No one else, no, no one else
Knows *that* as well as you!

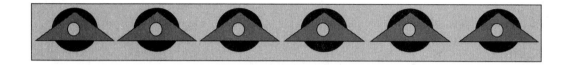

COMPREHENSION EXERCISE

1. In one or two sentences, summarize the main point of the poem.

2. List several kinds of things, according to the poem, that a person can learn from other people.

TOPICS FOR DISCUSSION OR WRITING

1. Interview a classmate about some of his or her favorite things. Take notes so you can recount some of them to the rest of the class. For example:
   ▼ A favorite food?
   ▼ Favorite clothes?
   ▼ A favorite activity?
   ▼ A favorite television show or movie?
   ▼ A special gift received?
   ▼ A favorite relative (family member)?
2. Think of a subject on which you and another person have disagreed. What were the different sides, and why did you feel as you did?
3. If you think back over some of the major "lessons" that you have learned in your life that have guided your decisions and actions, what would be one of them? From whom or how did you learn it? Write about this "guiding truth."

SECTION 4

PREREADING

List some of the rules and regulations you had to follow when you were growing up. Were there some rules that you disagreed with or felt were unfair? Take a few minutes and write about your feelings. You may want to share your ideas with a classmate, your teacher, or the whole class. If you prefer, write your answer in your private journal.

The story that follows is by Jamaica Kincaid, a writer who was born in St. Johns, Antigua. Antigua is an island in the Caribbean Sea. The story is written in a different style: it reads like a list or a stream of thoughts, one after another, as the narrator thinks about what she has been taught about how to act and who to be.

GIRL
Jamaica Kincaid

Wash the white clothes on Monday and put them on the stone heap; wash the color clothes on Tuesday and put them on the clothesline to dry; don't walk barehead in the hot sun; cook pumpkin fritters in very hot sweet oil; soak your little cloths right
5 after you take them off; when buying cotton to make yourself a nice blouse, be sure that it doesn't have gum in it, because that way it won't hold up well after a wash; soak salt fish overnight before you cook it; is it true that you sing benna in Sunday school?; always eat your food in such a way that it won't turn
10 someone else's stomach; on Sundays try to walk like a lady and not like the slut you are so bent on becoming; don't sing benna

in Sunday school; you mustn't speak to wharf-rat boys, not even to give directions; don't eat fruits on the street—flies will follow you; *but I don't sing benna on Sundays at all and never in*

15 *Sunday school;* this is how to sew on a button; this is how to make a buttonhole for the button you have just sewed on; this is how to hem a dress when you see the hem coming down and so to prevent yourself from looking like the slut I know you are so bent on becoming; this is how you iron your father's khaki

20 shirt so that it doesn't have a crease; this is how you iron your father's khaki pants so that they don't have a crease; this is how you grow okra—far from the house, because okra tree harbors red ants; when you are growing dasheen, make sure it gets plenty of water or else it makes your throat itch when you are

25 eating it; this is how you sweep a corner; this is how you sweep a whole house; this is how you sweep a yard; this is how you smile to someone you don't like too much; this is how you smile to someone you don't like at all; this is how you smile to someone you like completely; this is how you set a table for tea;

30 this is how you set a table for dinner; this is how you set a table for dinner with an important guest; this is how you set a table

for lunch; this is how you set a table for breakfast; this is how to
behave in the presence of men who don't know you very well,
and this way they won't recognize the slut I have warned you
35 against becoming; be sure to wash every day, even if it is with
your own spit; don't squat down to play marbles—you are not a
boy, you know; don't pick people's flowers—you might catch
something; don't throw stones at blackbirds, because it might
not be a blackbird at all; this is how to make bread pudding;
40 this is how to make doukona; this is how to make pepper pot;
this is how to make a good medicine for a cold; this is how to
make a good medicine to throw away a child before it even
becomes a child; this is how to catch a fish; this is how to throw
back a fish you don't like, and that way something bad won't
45 fall on you; this is how to bully a man; this is how a man bullies
you; this is how to love a man, and if this doesn't work there are
other ways, and if they don't work don't feel too bad about
giving up; this is how to spit up in the air if you feel like it, and
this is how to move quick so that it doesn't fall on you; this is
50 how to make ends meet; always squeeze bread to make sure
it's fresh; *but what if the baker won't let me feel the bread?*; you
mean to say that after all you are really going to be the kind of
woman who the baker won't let near the bread?

COMPREHENSION QUESTIONS

1. In a paragraph, sum up how you think the speaker feels about her life.

2. Describe the narrator's role in relation to others in the family.

3. Discuss the ending of the story: Who is talking in the italicized sentence, "*but what if the baker won't let me feel the bread?*" (line 51) Whose voice responds? What is the meaning of this exchange?

4. Whose voice is coming through in threatening that the narrator is "bent on becoming a slut"? What do you think the narrator means when she says this line?

TOPICS FOR DISCUSSION OR WRITING

Several of the topics listed next (especially those in 2, 4, and 6) lend themselves to a class debate between students who are on one side of the question and those who are on the other side. Another option is for students to pair up and debate with each other, either orally or in writing, by exchanging comments and reactions back and forth.

1. Think about a responsibility or chore that you hope that you never have to do again. What do you especially dislike about it?
2. Do you think a man could have written this story about himself? Why or why not?
3. If you are a man, would you trade places with the narrator in the story? Why or why not? If you are a woman, do you identify with her? Why or why not?
4. Do you think females can do these chores and handle these responsibilities better than men and *should* be doing them?
5. Describe the type of man or woman you were "supposed" to be like when you grew up. What were your family's expectations for you? How do you feel about these expectations?

6. How would you describe the traditional female role in your culture? The typical male role? Have these role expectations changed over the last few years?

7. If you had a son or daughter, what rules would you require them to follow? Would some of these rules be different for boys and girls?

SECTION 5

PREREADING

Do you know anyone who has suffered because of his or her political beliefs? What were the circumstances? Take a few minutes and write about your feelings. You may want to share your ideas with a classmate, your teacher, or the whole class. If you prefer, write your answer in your private journal.

Sometimes, politics affect who we are and how we live our lives. Many people live in countries where they are not able to be what they want to be because the political reality in their countries forces them to be something else. This seems to be what has happened to the speaker in the poem by the Vietnamese poet, Tru Vu.

WHO AM I?
Tru Vu

I am neither a communist
nor a nationalist:
I am Vietnamese.
Is it not enough?
5   For thousands of years
that's what I've been:
Don't you think that's enough?
And Vietnam in flames
and mother who weeps
10   and youngsters who suffer
and all the terminology we use to kill each other!
O river
we stand on our respective banks
our fallen tears mingling.

"Who Am I?" by Tru Vu from A THOUSAND YEARS OF VIETNAMESE POETRY. Copyright © 1975 by The Asia Society.

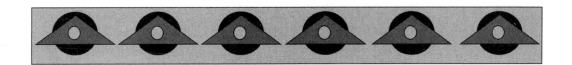

COMPREHENSION QUESTIONS

1. The speaker is "neither a communist nor a nationalist." What is he or she?

2. Why is Vietnam in flames?

3. Why does the mother weep?

4. Why do the youngsters suffer?

5. A river divides the north from the south in Vietnam. What do the last two lines mean: "we stand on our respective banks / our fallen tears mingling"? Are there examples in your own country's history of this situation?

6. What does the author mean by the line "all the terminology we use to kill each other"?

TOPICS FOR DISCUSSION OR WRITING

1. Complete the phrases that follow with three different responses about yourself. Don't just say the obvious. Think about what makes you different from others.

I am _____.

I am _____.

I am _____.

I am not _____.

I am not _____.

I am not _____.

2. The war in Vietnam has caused great suffering and displacement of people. Can you explain what happened in Vietnam before and after 1975? You may need to do some research or interview people to find out about Vietnam's history over the last 20 or so years. You also might find some disagreement in these explanations.

3. What are some of your political beliefs? Do you feel free to express them? Have you experienced a time when you did not feel free to express your political opinions?

4. The terms *liberal* and *conservative* are frequently used in the media to represent different political positions. What do you think is the difference between them? Which position do you have more in common with?

SECTION 6

PREREADING

> Do you think it is unusual for a woman to live alone—or to *want* to live alone? Take a few minutes and write about your feelings. You may want to share your ideas with a classmate, your teacher, or the whole class. If you prefer, write your answer in your private journal.

Our fantasies and hopes for the future are as much a part of our identity as our past and present experiences and emotions. Often these dreams for ourselves form a picture in our minds, though it may not be a picture that we reveal to others. In the passage by Sandra Cisneros, the narrator's hopes and dreams for herself are summed up in one particular image.

A HOUSE OF MY OWN
by Sandra Cisneros

Not a flat. Not an apartment in back. Not a man's house. Not a daddy's. A house all my own. With my porch and my pillow, my pretty purple petunias. My books and my stories. My two shoes waiting beside the bed. Nobody to shake a stick at.

5 Nobody's garbage to pick up after.

Only a house quiet as snow, a space for myself to go, clean as paper before the poem.

COMPREHENSION QUESTIONS

1. In a sentence, sum up the main point of the story.

2. Without looking back at the story, list three to four types of places the narrator does *not* want to live.

3. Why do you think that having a house of her own is so important to the narrator? What kind of living arrangements might she have experienced in her life to make her want this so much? Support your responses with references from the story.

TOPICS FOR DISCUSSION OR WRITING

1. If you could talk with the narrator and ask her any questions, what would you ask?
2. Describe a dream or goal you have for yourself and why it is important to you. You could try to write about it in the form of a poem, and also draw or paint what your dream looks and feels like.
3. People are complex and have different sides to themselves. Write a dialogue between two different sides of yourself—two voices inside of you, for example, representing

    {a} a lazy and a responsible you,
    {b} a strong and a weak you, or
    {c} an older and a younger self.

UNIT 2 MEMORIES

The theme of this unit is MEMORIES. Memories affect who we are, how we think about our lives, and how we interpret new experiences. Usually, the older we get, the more important our memories become to us. They can be triggered by a photograph, a smell, a particular piece of music; and it's often difficult to translate memory into words. Yet each of us has a rich treasure of memories from our past that is ours and ours alone. Socrates said: "The unexamined life is not worth living." What do you think he meant?

As you read the selections in this unit, recollect past experiences that are special to you. What is your earliest memory and how old were you? Is there a song that calls up a particular experience when you hear it? Do you have an old photograph of yourself or someone you love that brings back memories for you?

Some of the topics for discussion and writing that follow the readings may be ones that you would like to include in a personal notebook of your writings and poems. You may also include pictures or photographs with these entries or make drawings to go with them.

SECTION 1

PREREADING

Bring back some of your memories through your five senses: Describe a smell you remember, a sound you recall, the feel of something, a taste you remember, and something you saw. Try to find just the right words to capture these sensations. You may want to share your ideas with a classmate, your teacher, or the whole class. If you prefer, write your answer in your private journal.

The first reading is a true story written by Valerie Whiteson that recalls her childhood experience growing up in South Africa. The story reveals that children and parents may see the same situation very differently.

GOLDFIELDS HOTEL
Valerie Whiteson

One of the reasons we left South Africa was because of the time I told my son Mark to pick up his toys and he turned to me and said with all the wisdom of a four-year-old, "I don't have to pick up things. I haven't got brown hands!"

5   When I was four years old, I hadn't noticed that people of different colors were treated differently. We lived in a cottage in the yard of my parent's hotel in the northern Transvaal. Apart from the barmen who were white, all the other workers were Indians or Africans, but then they were called Natives.

10   The waiters were all Indians and I thought they were very handsome men. They had shiny, wet-looking black hair and smooth brown polished skins. They also had a different smell from other people I knew. As far as I can tell now, it must have been curry.

15   They spoke a different language, too, which I couldn't
understand. People used to make fun of their sing-song accents
in English. Much later in life when I went to Wales and heard
people speaking, they sounded exactly like the Indian waiters
of my childhood. All the waiters spoiled me. They were ready to
20   bring me an extra ice cream after my parents had left the
dining room.
      Flora, my nanny, was an African. Her skin was a shiny
brown and her hair was always covered. I still don't know why.
Her teeth were very clean and white, although she didn't have
25   a toothbrush. She too smelled funny and her hands were
different.
      The palms were light-colored and rough. She dressed me,
bathed me, and took me for walks. She had great patience and
in many ways was as close to me as my mother. I never could
30   understand why my parents told me not to go to her room. The
Africans lived in bare rooms at the back of the hotel. One day I
disobeyed and went to her room.
      It was very cold. The floor was cement, polished red with floor
polish, which you could smell. The iron bed was much higher
35   than mine since it was set on tin cans to raise it up from the
floor. This was so that Tokoloshi wouldn't be able to get her.
Flora wouldn't tell me who Tokoloshi was, but I imagined him to
be like Wee Willie Winkie, who terrified me. The bed was
covered by a starched, pure white bedspread. On the pillow
40   there was a hand-embroidered pillow slip covered with red,
orange, and yellow flowers, birds, and butterflies. There was a
candle in a bottle on the floor and that was all. There was
nothing to be afraid of, so I started going there often.
      My best time to visit was when the servants were going to
45   eat. There was nothing I liked better than their food. Just
thinking about it "makes the water to run in my mouth" as one
of my nannies used to say.
      They always ate exactly the same food every day and I
loved to eat with them. First they would cook unrefined corn
50   meal in water till it was so thick that you could dip your fingers
in the pot, then take some out and roll it into a lump. They
called it *stywe mealie pap* which is Afrikaans for "thick
cornmeal porridge." The pap is dipped into a meaty gravy and
eaten with your fingers. It was delicious and to this day I long
55   for it. On special occasions they would eat meat too. In South
Africa white housewives still order "Boy's Meat." It's a cheap cut,
which is hard and stringy, but then it tasted much better than

any meat my parents ate and enjoyed in the hotel dining room.

60 The pap was cooked in a black bellied, cast-iron pot with three legs which is called a kaffir-pot. It was placed over an open wood fire, and we all squatted around it. When the pap was ready, the cook would put down the wooden stick used to stir it and invite us to eat. The Africans could touch the boiling hot porridge, but I would have to wait for it to cool. Each person

65 had a battered tin plate and no spoons, knives, or forks. I loved the way we ate. Nobody said anything about table manners. Gravy was poured into the tin platters and we licked our fingers after eating the lump of pap, which had been dipped in the gravy.

70 Squatting in the circle listening to them chatting away in a language I could not understand, I was innocently happy. Unfortunately my happiness didn't last long.

My father came looking for the garden boy. When he saw me squatting there with the servants, he was horrified. He

75 picked me up and carried me away screaming. He promised to spank me if he ever caught me eating with the servants again. I didn't understand, but I had learned the same lesson my son was to learn. The truth is that I never went back.

VOCABULARY EXERCISE

From the list below, choose the word that makes sense in each sentence. Write the word in the blank. Try each one without looking back at the story, then check your answers. You may have to change the form of the word.

hand-embroidered	(line 40)	squat	(line 61)
		polished	(line 12)
horrify	(line 74)	innocent	(line 71)
patience	(line 28)	spoil	(line 19)
chat	(line 70)	imagined	(line 37)

1. The waiters _____ me by giving me extra ice

   cream after my parents left the dining room after dinner.

2. They had smooth brown _____ skins.

3. On the pillow in Flora's room there was a

   _____ pillow slip covered with red, orange

   and yellow flowers, birds, and butterflies.

4. My nanny, Flora, was very _____ with me as

   she tended to me.

5. I _____ Tokoloshi was like Wee Willie Winkie

   in the nursery rhyme.

6. I listened to them _____ away in an African

   language that I didn't understand.

7. I felt _____ and happy when I

_____ in the circle around the fire and ate

dinner with the servants.

8. When my father walked in and saw me with the servants, he was

_____.

COMPREHENSION QUESTIONS

1. Why do you think the hotel is called "Goldfields"? (Clue: Recall the country where the story took place.)

2. Why do the narrator's parents forbid her from going to the servants' rooms?

3. Why can't she understand the language spoken by the Indians and the Africans?

4. Why does the narrator enjoy eating with the servants?

5. Why does her father threaten to spank her?

6. What lesson do the narrator and her own son Mark learn?

TOPICS FOR DISCUSSION OR WRITING

1. Was there a special place or person that you were attracted to as a child that was off-limits to you? If so, write about that experience. Why was it interesting to you, and why was it off-limits?

2. Did you do something as a child that made your parents angry? As you look back on it now, who do you think was right—you, your parents, or both of you?

3. Do you identify more with the girl in the story or with her father in regard to her relationship with the servants? (It would be interesting for classmates on opposing sides of this question to debate each other.)

4. Do you think it is possible to grow up in a racist society and *not* be racist yourself? Explain.

WRITING STRATEGY LESSON: DESCRIPTIVE LANGUAGE

Even for professional writers, finding just the right word to capture the character of a person, the mood of a place, or the essence of an experience can be a challenge. Nevertheless, they strive to find words that are not overused and are fresh and vivid for the reader. The reader should be able to see and feel the experience being described. The author of "Goldfields Hotel" uses descriptive language to help you experience her childhood memory. She uses very specific, concrete words to express what she saw, heard, felt, and even smelled. For example, in the third paragraph, she depicts the waiters as having "shiny, wet-looking black hair and smooth brown polished skins." (line 11) They also smell of curry. Can you see and smell what she experienced?

Skim back over the story and underline at least five words or phrases that are particularly effective for you in understanding her experience. Share these with your classmates.

The next three sentences are grammatically correct, but they are boring. Rewrite them so they express a feeling, a mood, and a sensation in a fresher, more original way.

1. The baby is happy.

The _____

2. The rain was loud.

The _____

3. The fruit tasted sweet.

The _____

SECTION 2

PREREADING

Do you think that there are any places in the world where people are accepted without regard to the color of their skin? Would you like to live in such a place? Write your answer to these questions. You may want to share your ideas with a classmate, your teacher, or the whole class. If you prefer, write your answer in your private journal.

Some countries have a completely different attitude toward color. People who come from Puerto Rico, for example, may have grown up feeling like the narrator in Tato Laviera's poem "Boricua." The title of this poem refers to the people who originally inhabited Puerto Rico.

BORICUA
Tato Laviera

we are a people
who love to love
we are loving
lovers who love
5   to love respect,
the best intentions
of friendship,
and we judge from
the moment on, no
10 matter who you are,
and, if we find
sincere smiles,
we can be friends,
and, if we have a
15 drink together,
we can be brothers,
on the spot, no
matter who you are,
and we have a lot
20 of black & white
& yellow & red
people whom we
befriend, we're
ready to love
25 with you, that's
why we
say, let there
be no prejudice,
on race, color is
30 generally color-blind
with us, that's our
contribution, all
the colors are tied
to our one,

35 but we must fight
the bad intentions,
we must respect
each other's values,
but guess what,
40 we're not the only ones,
and we offer what your
love has taught us,
and what you're worth
in our self-respect,
45 we are a people
who love to love
who are loving
lovers who love
to love respect.

"Boricua" is reprinted from *American. Copyright* ©1985 with permission of Arte Público Press.

VOCABULARY EXERCISE

Complete these sentences with a word listed below from the poem.
You may have to change the form of the word to fit the particular
sentence structure.

contribution	(line 32)	value	(line 38)
befriend	(line 23)	sincere	(line 12)
offer	(line 41)	respect	(line 05)
intention	(line 06)	prejudice	(line 28)
judge	(line 08)	color-blind	(line 30)

1. My daughter got angry with me because I asked her boyfriend
   about his _____ toward her.

2. Do you _____ my right to disagree with you?

3. If you are honest and _____, you will have lots
   of friends.

4. _____ and biased people are their own worst
   enemies.

5. I will never forget the first person who _____
   me when I first arrived in this country.

6. More men than women are _____. They can't
   tell the difference between blue and green.

7. Most people make a _____ to charity from
   time to time.

8. It's very difficult to teach a child good _____.

   The best way to do it is by setting an example.

9. Children should be taught good _____.

10. When I went to my teacher's house, he _____

    me a cup of tea.

COMPREHENSION QUESTIONS

1. What kind of people does the poet describe?

2. What quality do they look for in strangers so that they can befriend them?

3. When they look at people of different colors, what do they see?

4. What does it mean to be "color-blind" literally? How is the speaker also using the term figuratively as a metaphor?

5. How does this attitude to strangers affect the self-respect of the people in the poem?

TOPICS FOR DISCUSSION OR WRITING

1. Do you know people who are color-blind—in the metaphoric sense? Why do you think some people adopt this value, and others become prejudiced and judgmental about people of a different skin color?

2. What is or was your family's attitude toward people who are different from them, for example, people of a different color or religion? How were these attitudes communicated to you—directly or through their actions?

3. What values about people of a different color, religion, or culture do you hope to teach or pass on to your children? How do you plan to do this?

SECTION 3

PREREADING

What was the best and worst thing about being sick when you were a child? Take a few minutes and write down a memory of being sick. Remember to strive to find vivid words to recapture the experience. You may want to share your ideas with a classmate, your teacher, or the whole class. If you prefer, write your answer in your private journal.

The next story is also about childhood. It is written by Ernest Hemingway about a boy who has a bad experience because he does not fully understand what is happening to him. Has that ever happened to you? As you read the story, recall memories of times when you were sick as a child.

A DAY'S WAIT
Ernest Hemingway

He came into the room to shut the windows while we were still in bed, and I saw he looked ill. He was shivering, his face was white, and he walked slowly as though it ached to move.

"What's the matter, Schatz?"

5   "I've got a headache."

"You better go back to bed."

"No. I'm all right."

"You go to bed. I'll see you when I'm dressed."

But when I came downstairs he was dressed, sitting by the

10 fire, looking a very sick and miserable boy of nine years. When I put my hand on his forehead I knew he had a fever.

"You go up to bed," I said, "you're sick."

"I'm all right," he said.

When the doctor came he took the boy's temperature.

15 "What is it?" I asked him.

"One hundred and two."

Downstairs, the doctor left three different medicines in different colored capsules with instructions for giving them. One was to bring down the fever, another a purgative, the third to

20 overcome an acid condition. The germs of influenza can exist only in an acid condition, he explained. He seemed to know all

about influenza and said there was nothing to worry about if the fever did not go above one hundred and four degrees. This was a light epidemic of flu, and there was no danger if you

25 avoided pneumonia.

Back in the room I wrote down the boy's temperature and made a note of the time to give the various capsules.

"Do you want me to read to you?"

"All right. If you want to," said the boy. His face was very

30 white and there were dark areas under his eyes. He lay still in the bed and seemed very detached from what was going on.

I read aloud from Howard Pyle's *Book of Pirates*; but I could see he was not following what I was reading.

"How do you feel, Schatz?" I asked him.

35   "Just the same, so far," he said.

I sat at the foot of the bed and read to myself while I waited for it to be time to give another capsule. It would have been natural for him to go to sleep, but when I looked up he was looking at the foot of the bed, looking very strangely.

40   "Why don't you try to go to sleep? I'll wake you up for the medicine."

"I'd rather stay awake."

After a while he said to me, "You don't have to stay in here with me, Papa, if it bothers you."

45   "It doesn't bother me."

"No, I mean you don't have to stay if it's going to bother you."

I thought perhaps he was a little light-headed, and after giving him the prescribed capsules at eleven o'clock I went out for a while. It was a bright, cold day, the ground covered with a

50   sleet that had frozen so that it seemed as if all the bare trees, the bushes, the cut brush and all the grass and the bare ground had been varnished with ice. I took the young Irish setter for a little walk up the road and along a frozen creek, but it was difficult to stand or walk on the glass surface, and the red dog

55   slipped and slithered and I fell twice, hard, once dropping my gun and having it slide away over the ice.

We flushed a covey of quail under a high clay bank with overhanging brush, and I killed two as they went out of sight over the top of the bank. Some of the covey lit in trees, but most

60   of them scattered into brush piles; and it was necessary to jump on the ice-coated mounds of brush several times before they would flush. Coming out while you were poised unsteadily on the icy, springy brush, they made difficult shooting and I killed two, missed five, and started back pleased to have found a

65   covey close to the house and happy there were so many left to find on another day.

At the house they said the boy had refused to let anyone come into the room.

"You can't come in," he said. "You mustn't get what I have."

70   I went up to him and found him in exactly the position I had left him, white-faced, but with the tops of his cheeks flushed by the fever, staring still, as he had stared, at the foot of the bed.

I took his temperature.

"What is it?"

75   "Something like a hundred," I said. It was one hundred and two and four-tenths.

"It was a hundred and two," he said.

"Who said so?"

"The doctor."

80   "Your temperature is all right," I said. "It's nothing to worry about."

"I don't worry," he said, "but I can't keep from thinking."

"Don't think," I said. "Just take it easy."

"I'm taking it easy," he said and looked straight ahead. He

85 was evidently holding tight onto himself about something.

"Take this with water."

"Do you think it will do any good?"

"Of course it will."

I sat down and opened the *Pirate* book and commenced to

90 read, but I could see he was not following, so I stopped.

"About what time do you think I'm going to die?" he asked.

"What?"

"About how long will it be before I die?"

"You aren't going to die. What's the matter with you?"

95   "Oh, yes, I am. I heard him say a hundred and two."

"People don't die with a fever of one hundred and two. That's a silly way to talk."

"I know they do. At school in France the boys told me you can't live with forty-four degrees. I've got a hundred and two."

100   He had been waiting to die all day, ever since nine o'clock in the morning.

"You poor Schatz," I said. "Poor old Schatz. It's like miles and kilometers. You aren't going to die. That's a different thermometer. On that thermometer thirty-seven is normal. On

105 this kind it's ninety-eight."

"Are you sure?"

"Absolutely," I said. "It's like miles and kilometers. You know, like how many kilometers we make when we do seventy miles in the car?"

110   "Oh," he said.

But his gaze at the foot of the the bed relaxed slowly, the hold over himself relaxed too, finally, and the next day it was very slack and he cried very easily at little things that were of no importance.

VOCABULARY EXERCISE

Match the first part of the sentence (A) with the second part (B) so that it makes sense:

A

1. Come in and change your wet clothes . . .

2. The girl became *flushed*. . .

3. He absolutely *refused* to take his medicine, . . .

4. I asked the doctor what he had *prescribed* . . .

5. You must wash your hands before you eat . . .

6. Let's stop working now and *relax* . . .

7. My back *aches* . . .

8. Many people died . . .

B

a. for my mother's illness.

b. from working at the computer too long.

c. because you are *shivering*.

d. when there was a flu *epidemic*.

e. thus his *pain* got worse.

f. when the famous movie star spoke to her.

g. for awhile.

h. otherwise the *germs* will make you sick.

COMPREHENSION EXERCISE

Complete the sentences so that they make sense according to the story.

Schatz had a (1) _____ because he had influenza

(the flu). The (2) _____ came and told the boy

and his father that Schatz's (3) _____ was 102

degrees. The doctor left three types of (4) _____

in different colored capsules with (5) _____

about when to take them. The father went hunting with his red dog and

shot two (6) _____; when he came back,

Schatz was sitting in exactly the same (7) _____

as he was before his father left. Schatz asked his father (8) "_____

_____ ?"

He had been (9) _____ all day to die because

he heard the boys at school say that people die if their temperature (10)

_____ 44 degrees, and his was 102.

COMPREHENSION QUESTIONS

1. Who is the narrator of the story? How do you know?

2. Why does Schatz think he is going to die?

3. Which scale, Centigrade or Fahrenheit, does the doctor use? Which scale does Schatz think in terms of? How does Schatz's father explain the difference between these two scales for measuring temperature? Which one are you most familiar with?

4. How does Schatz react to the possibility of his death?

TOPICS FOR DISCUSSION OR WRITING

1. Interview someone (a classmate, friend, or family member) about a time when that person was sick as a child. What does he or she remember most?

2. In the story, the father reads Schatz a story about pirates. When you were sick as a child, did your parents read to you? In your culture, do parents generally read aloud to their children? What do you think about this practice?

3. In your opinion, who do you think make better patients—males or females? Why? Who do you think make better nurses—males or females? Why?

4. Can you recall a particular fear you had as a child? How did your family react to your fear (if they knew about it)? Write about this memory from the point of view of yourself as a child.

5. The following is a list of some of the typical fears that children have. Did you have any of these fears? Put a + if you were afraid of it, and a – if you were not. Write in any other fears you might have had. After doing this exercise, compare your responses to those of your classmates.

Were you afraid of . . .

_____ **a.** the dark?

_____ **b.** being alone at home?

_____ **c.** earthquakes (or other natural disasters)?

_____ **d.** snakes?

_____ **e.** insects, such as _____?

_____ **f.** the "bogey man"—someone who would sneak up on you and

scare you? What did this creature look like? Could you describe

or draw it?

_____ **g.** a place that was scary? Can you describe it?

_____ **h.** a person who was scary? Can you describe him or her?

_____ **i.** a dream image or nightmare you have had?

_____ **j.** other fears?

SECTION 4

PREREADING

Do you recall a memory told to you by one of your older relatives or friends—perhaps from a time when they were younger and/or lived in another country? Spend a few minutes writing it down. You may want to share your ideas with a classmate, your teacher, or the whole class. If you prefer, write your answer in your private journal.

The next selection is a poem by Kitty Tsui. The speaker becomes the voice of her grandmother's memories. Her grandmother, Kwan Ying Lin, emigrated from China to the United States in 1922.

CHINATOWN TALKING STORY
Kitty Tsui

the gold mountain men said
there were two pairs of eyes
so beautiful
they had the power
5   to strike you dead,
the eyes of
kwan ying lin
and mao dan so.

kwan ying lin, my grandmother,
10   and mao dan so
were stars of the cantonese opera
and women
rare
in a bachelor society.

15   when my grandmother first came
to gold mountain in 1922
she was interned on angel island
for weeks, a young chinese girl,
prisoner in a strange land.

20   when mao dan so
first arrived
she came on an entertainer's visa
and made $10,000 a year.

it cost $1.25 to see a show,
25   a quarter after nine.
pork chop rice was $.15.

when theater work was slow
or closed down
other work was found:
30   washing dishes,
waiting tables, ironing shirts.

in china
families with sons
saved and borrowed
35   the $3,000
to buy a bright boy
promise in a new land.

in china
girls born into poverty
40   were killed or sold.
girls born into
prosperity
had their feet bound,
their marriages arranged.

45   on angel island
paper sons and blood sons
waited

to enter *gum san*
eating peanut butter on crackers
50 for lunch and
bean sprouts at night.

the chinamen who passed the interrogations
were finally set free.
the ones who failed
55 were denied entry and deported
or died by their own hands.

in 1940, the year
angel island detention center
was closed,
60 a job at macy's
paid $27 a week.
only chinese girls
without accents please apply.

my grandfather had four wives
65 and pursued many women
during his life.
the chinese press loved to write of his affairs.

my grandmother,
a woman with three daughters,
70 left her husband
to survive on her own.
she lived with another actress,
a companion and a friend.

the gold mountain men said
75 mao dan so was as graceful
as a peach blossom in wind.

she has worked since
she was eight.
she is seventy-two.
80 she sits in her apartment
in new york chinatown
playing solitaire.
her hair is thin and white.
her eyes, sunken in hollows,
85 are fire bright when she speaks.

the gold mountain men said
when kwan ying lin
went on stage
even the electric fans stopped.

90 today
at the grave
of my grandmother
with fresh spring flowers,
iris, daffodil,
95 i felt her spirit in the wind.
i heard her voice saying:

born into the
skin of yellow women
we are born
100 into the armor of warriors.

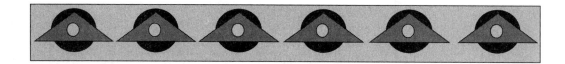

VOCABULARY EXERCISE

From the choices provided, choose the best word to complete the sentence. The words are similar in meaning, but there is one that fits better than the others to accurately convey the meaning of the sentence.

1. The Chinese who came to America underwent _____.

    a. third degrees   **b.** demands   **c.** quizzes   **d.** interrogation

2. Only a few Chinese gained _____.

    a. luxury   **b.** abundance   **c.** prosperity   **d.** money

3. Many were _____ back to their homeland.

    a. imported   **b.** deported   **c.** immigrated   **d.** expelled

4. Sometimes it is difficult for a new immigrant to adjust to the new

    _____.

    a. society   **b.** group   **c.** culture   **d.** civilization

5. A few immigrants live in a state of _____.

    a. poverty   **b.** necessity   **c.** poorness   **d.** inadequacy

6. The poem is about people who are brave and overcome

    _____.

    a. disaster   **b.** luck   **c.** hardships   **d.** pressures

COMPREHENSION EXERCISE

Complete the sentences according to the information in the poem.

1. Kwan Ying Lin and Mao Dan So were _____

_____.

2. Kwan Ying Lin is the speaker's _____.

3. Kwan Ying Lin came to the United States in _____ and hoped

to get work as _____.

4. When the theater work was slow or closed down, she found other

work, such as _____

and _____.

5. In China, girls born of poor families were _____

_____.

6. In China, girls born of rich families had _____

_____.

7. Kwan Ying Lin worked since she was _____ years old.

8. Kwan Ying Lin left her husband because _____

_____.

COMPREHENSION QUESTIONS

1. Who are the gold mountain men living in a bachelor society?

2. What does Mao Dan So do when she comes to the United States?
   How much money does she make?

3. What other work experiences do the two women have in the United States, and how does the money compare to Mao Dan So's income as an entertainer?

4. What point do you think that the speaker is making about the working conditions of Chinese immigrants, especially women?

5. What examples of discrimination against Asian Americans are referred to in the poem?

6. What is the meaning of the last lines of the poem: "born into the / skin of yellow women / we are born / into the armor of warriors"?

7. What are some similarities and differences between the discrimination against Africans and Indians in the story *Goldfields Hotel* and the Asians in this poem?

8. How were girl children (both rich and poor) and boy children treated in China? Why do you think these customs existed?

WRITING STRATEGY ACTIVITIES

1. Find at least one example of a metaphor in the poem and one example of a simile.
2. The writer describes a unique time and place in the lives of two women and how they were affected by their extraordinary situation. Her picture is very moving. One language strategy that contributes to the impact of the poem is the use of concrete imagery. Look back over the poem and underline specific words and phrases that enhance your ability to imagine what the author is talking about.

TOPICS FOR DISCUSSION OR WRITING

1. If you are an immigrant yourself or if you have made a major move in your life, what were some of your expectations about your new home? What kind of life (and work) did you picture for yourself? (You may also choose to interview someone else who has experienced such a move and ask him or her these questions.)
2. The reference to an ad for work at Macy's Department Store (lines 60-63) indicates that they would not hire Chinese girls with accents. How do you feel about this policy? Do you agree or disagree with it?
3. Interview an Asian American who might know about Chinese customs related to treating female children differently from male children. Ask this person why these customs were established and if the customs have changed over the years. Also, ask whether he or she has had any first-hand experience with these customs. (If no Asian-Americans are available for such an interview, select someone from another culture and ask about differences in the treatment of girls and boys in that person's culture.)

SECTION 5

PREREADING

Think about something that embarrassed you when you were a child; for example, a garment or a haircut you disliked. Write a letter to the person who was responsible for this humiliation—a parent or family member, a teacher, or a friend. Try to capture the experience and your feelings vividly, as though you were watching a scene from a movie. You may want to share your ideas with a classmate, your teacher, or the whole class. If you prefer, write your answer in your private journal.

The final story in this unit is by Gary Soto, who often writes about his experiences as a Latino growing up in California. In this story the narrator remembers how difficult it was to be poor.

THE JACKET
Gary Soto

My clothes have failed me. I remember the green coat that I wore in fifth and sixth grades when you either danced like a champ or pressed yourself against a greasy wall, bitter as a penny toward the happy couples.

5   When I needed a new jacket and my mother asked what kind I wanted, I described something like bikers wear: black leather and silver studs with enough belts to hold down a small town. We were in the kitchen, steam on the windows from her cooking. She listened so long while stirring dinner that I thought

10 she understood for sure the kind I wanted. The next day when I
got home from school, I discovered draped on my bedpost a
jacket the color of day-old guacamole. I threw my books on the
bed and approached the jacket slowly, as if it were a stranger
whose hand I had to shake. I touched the vinyl sleeve, the
15 collar, and peeked at the mustard-colored lining.
    From the kitchen mother yelled that my jacket was in the
closet. I closed the door to her voice and pulled at the rack of
clothes in the closet, hoping the jacket on the bedpost wasn't for
me but my mean brother. No luck. I gave up. From my bed, I
20 stared at the jacket. I wanted to cry because it was so ugly and
so big that I knew I'd have to wear it a long time. I was a small
kid, thin as a young tree, and it would be years before I'd have
a new one. I stared at the jacket, like an enemy, thinking bad
things before I took off my old jacket whose sleeves climbed
25 halfway to my elbow.
    I put the big jacket on. I zipped it up and down several times,
and rolled the cuffs up so that they didn't cover my hands. I put
my hands in the pockets and flapped the jacket like a bird's
wings. I stood in front of the mirror, full face, then profile, and
30 then looked over my shoulder as if someone had called me. I
sat on the bed, stood against the bed, and combed my hair to
see what I would look like doing something natural. I looked
ugly. I threw it on my brother's bed and looked at it for a long
time before I slipped it on and went out to the backyard,
35 smiling a "thank you" to my mom as I passed her in the kitchen.
With my hands in my pockets I kicked a ball against the fence,
and then climbed it to sit looking into the alley. I hurled orange
peels at the mouth of an open garbage can and when the peels
were gone I watched the white puffs of my breath thin to
40 nothing.
    I jumped down, hands in my pockets, and in the backyard
on my knees I teased my dog, Brownie, by swooping my arms
while making bird calls. He jumped at me and missed. He
jumped again and again, until a tooth sunk deep, ripping an L-
45 shaped tear on my left sleeve. I pushed Brownie away to study
the tear as I would a cut on my arm. There was no blood, only
a few loose pieces of fuzz. Damn dog, I thought, and pushed
him away hard as he tried to bite again. I got up from my
knees and went to my bedroom to sit with my jacket on my lap,
50 with the lights out.

That was the first afternoon with my new jacket. The next day I wore it to sixth grade and got a D on a math quiz. During the morning recess Frankie T., the playground terrorist, pushed me to the ground and told me to stay there until recess was

55 over. My best friend, Steve Negrete, ate an apple while looking at me, and the girls turned away to whisper on the monkey bars. The teachers were no help: they looked my way and talked about how foolish I looked in my new jacket. I saw their heads bob with laughter, their hands half-covering their

60 mouths.

Even though it was cold, I took off the jacket during lunch and played kickball in a thin shirt, my arms feeling like braille from goose bumps. But when I returned to class I slipped the jacket on and shivered until I was warm. I sat on my hands,

65 heating them up, while my teeth chattered like a cup of crooked dice. Finally warm, I slid out of the jacket but a few minutes later put it back on when the fire bell rang. We paraded out into the yard where we, the fifth graders, walked past all the other grades to stand against the back fence.

70 Everybody saw me. Although they didn't say out loud, "Man, that's ugly," I heard the buzz-buzz of gossip and even laughter that I knew was meant for me.

And so I went, in my guacamole jacket. So embarrassed, so hurt, I couldn't even do my homework. I received Cs on quizzes,

75 and forgot the state capitals and the rivers of South America, our friendly neighbor. Even the girls who had been friendly blew away like loose flowers to follow the boys in neat jackets.

I wore that thing for three years until the sleeves grew short and my forearms stuck out like the necks of turtles. All during

80 that time no love came to me — no little dark girl in a Sunday dress she wore on Monday. At lunchtime I stayed with the ugly boys who leaned against the chainlink fence and looked around with propellors of grass spinning in our mouths. We saw girls walk by alone, saw couples, hand in hand, their heads like

85 bookends pressing air together. We saw them and spun our propellors so fast our faces were blurs.

I blame that jacket for those bad years. I blame my mother for her bad taste and her cheap ways. It was a sad time for the heart. With a friend I spent my sixth-grade year in a tree in the

90 alley, waiting for something good to happen to me in the jacket, which had become the ugly brother who tagged along wherever I went. And it was about that time that I began to

grow. My chest puffed up with muscle and, strangely, a few
more ribs. Even my hands, those fleshy hammers, showed
95 bravely through the cuffs, the fingers already hardening for the
coming fights. But that L-shaped rip on the left sleeve got
bigger; bits of stuffing coughed out from its wound after a hard
day of play. I finally scotch-taped it closed, but in rain or cold
weather the tape peeled off like a scab and more stuffing fell
100 out until that sleeve shriveled into a palsied arm. That winter
the elbows began to crack and whole chunks of green began to
fall off. I showed the cracks to my mother, who always seemed
to be at the stove with steamed-up glasses, and she said that
there were children in Mexico who would love that jacket. I told
105 her that this was America and yelled that Debbie, my sister,
didn't have a jacket like mine. I ran outside, ready to cry, and
climbed the tree by the alley to think bad thoughts and watch
my breath puff white and disappear.

But whole pieces still casually flew off my jacket when I
110 played hard, read quietly, or took vicious spelling tests at
school. When it became so spotted that my brother began to
call me "camouflage," I flung it over the fence into the alley.
Later, however, I swiped the jacket off the ground and went
inside to drape it across my lap and mope.
115 I was called to dinner: steam silvered my mother's glasses as
she said grace; my brother and sister with their heads bowed
made ugly faces at their glasses of powdered milk. I gagged
too, but eagerly ate big rips of buttered tortilla that held
scooped up beans. Finished, I went outside with my jacket
120 across my arm. It was a cold sky. The faces of clouds were piled
up, hurting. I climbed the fence, jumping down with a grunt. I
started up the alley and soon slipped into my jacket, that green
ugly brother who breathed over my shoulder that day and ever
since.

VOCABULARY EXERCISE

Some of the words in the passage may have been new to you. Practice using some of the words from the story, which are listed below. Pay special attention to the form of the word: Some of them need to be changed to fit correctly into the sentence structure.

profile	(line 29)	blur	(line 86)
tease	(line 42)	cheaply	(line 88)
braille	(line 62)	tags	(line 91)
paraded	(line 68)	camouflage	(line 112)
embarass	(line 73)	gossip	(line 71)
neatly	(line 77)		

1. Fashion models and actors often believe that their right or left

   _____ is more photogenic when they have

   their pictures taken.

2. The little boy was _____ his sister about her

   new boyfriend.

3. Many blind people learn to read _____, a

   system of raised dots, felt and interpreted with the fingers.

4. On public holidays such as Thanksgiving and Independence Day,

   there is a _____ through the center of town.

5. Young people are often more _____ than their

   elders.

6. My uniform must be _____ and clean every

   day.

7. I can't see the screen without my contact lenses: Everything looks

_____.

8. Children are sometimes embarrassed when their parents (or

caretakers) buy them _____ clothes, but that

may be all they can afford.

9. "Go away! Go and play with your own friends. I don't want you to

_____ along with me."

10. Soldiers in battle often wear _____ uniforms

that help them blend in with the environment in order to hide from

the enemy.

11. People enjoy _____ about other people, even

though it can be very hurtful to the others and can even backfire

on the person who _____.

COMPREHENSION EXERCISE

Complete these sentences in your own words, according to the story.

1. He wanted a kind of coat that _____

_____.

2. The speaker describes the color of the jacket as _____

_____.

3. The two things wrong with the jacket are that it is too _____

and _____.

4. Brownie, the narrator's dog, _____

_____.

5. The next day at school, he had problems _____

_____.

6. The following day, he was still embarrassed and _____

_____.

7. The speaker wore the jacket for_____

_____.

8. He blames his mother for two things: _____

_____.

9. He spent most of the time during this period _____

_____.

COMPREHENSION QUESTIONS

1. Why is the narrator so embarrassed by the jacket? Why does he refer to it as "guacamole"?

2. If he detests the jacket so much, why does he continue to wear it?

3. Why does he blame the jacket for "those bad years"?

4. What does his brother mean when he calls him and the jacket "camouflage"?

WRITING STRATEGY ACTIVITIES

The most descriptive words in a sentence can be almost any part of speech. For example, they can be nouns, adjectives, verbs, or adverbs. Good writers often try to make their nouns concrete, their verbs active, and their adjectives and adverbs vivid. A couple of examples of the use of concrete nouns in "The Jacket" are the reference to the main character's classmate, Frankie T., as "the playground terrorist" in paragraph 6 and the phrase "the buzz-buzz of gossip" (line 71).

The author uses active verbs in the fourth paragraph when he writes that the character "*hurled* orange peels at the mouth of the open garbage can . . . " (italics added). (lines 37–38) In the same sentence, the reference to the garbage can's *mouth* is a creative choice of words that makes us see this commonplace object through a child's eyes as he humanizes an inanimate object. And there are numerous examples of vivid adjectives and adverbs, such as in his description of the jacket as "guacamole," rather than merely green; or of spelling tests as "vicious," rather than just difficult.

See if you can find several more examples of descriptive writing in the story. Underline your examples and see if you can also figure out what part of speech it is—noun, verb, adjective, or adverb.

The author is also extremely masterful in the use of metaphors and similes. Can you find at least three examples of each? Circle your examples.

TOPICS FOR DISCUSSION OR WRITING

1. What kinds of experiences are most embarrassing to young people? Why do you think these situations are so embarrassing?

2. In the prereading exercise, you were asked to write a letter to someone you felt had been responsible for an embarrassment that you experienced as a child. Now write a response to your letter from that person. (Their explanations and feelings can be imaginary, of course.)

3. If you could change one thing about your childhood, what would it be?

4. Write a descriptive paragraph about a garment, a room, or a neighborhood from your childhood. Try to capture the sensory aspects of the experience; and try to make your nouns concrete, your verbs active, and your adjectives and adverbs vivid.

UNIT 3 RELATIONSHIPS

Past experiences and relationships shape our identity. We establish different kinds of relationships all our lives—with family members, friends, co-workers, acquaintances, and sometimes even with strangers. Why are we attracted to certain people and uninterested or even repelled by others? And in what ways do our parents and childhood influence our adult relationships with others? Relationships can be loving or hurtful; they can bring out our best self or our worst self; they can be freeing or limiting. Even when relationships appear to others to be hurtful, individuals *in* the relationship may choose to stay in the relationship and pretend that nothing is wrong.

The readings in this unit describe different kinds of relationships—some loving, some hurtful—between former lovers, between mother and daughter, and between a husband and wife. As with the other units, you may find it especially meaningful to you to keep a personal notebook of some of your thoughts and writing assignments for the unit. Include pictures, photos, or drawings with your writings if you like.

SECTION 1

PREREADING

Describe someone you love. If you prefer, write a short poem of about four to six lines about this person. You may want to share your ideas with a classmate, your teacher, or the whole class. If you prefer, write your answer in your private journal.

In Gary Snyder's poem, "Seaman's Ditty," the speaker mourns a lost love. He wonders what might have happened had they stayed together and what his former lover is doing now. Have you ever had these kinds of thoughts about someone you knew earlier in your life?

SEAMAN'S DITTY
Gary Snyder

I'm wondering where you are now
Married, or mad, or free;
Wherever you are you're likely glad,
But memory troubles me.

5   We could've had us children,
We could've had a home—
But you thought not, and I thought not,
And these nine years we roam.

Today I worked in the deep dark tanks,
10   And climbed out to watch the sea;
Gulls and salty waves pass by,
And mountains of Araby.

I've traveled the lonely oceans
And wandered the lonely towns.
15   I've learned a lot and lost a lot,
And proved the world was round.

Now if we'd stayed together,
There's much we'd never've known—
But dreary books and weary lands
20   Weigh on me like a stone.

Indian Ocean

VOCABULARY EXERCISE

Complete these sentences with one of the words from the poem. You may have to change the form of the word.

weigh	(line 20)	roam	(line 08)
dreary	(line 19)	gull	(line 11)
troubles	(line 04)	weary	(line 19)
proves	(line 16)		

1. I have _____ the world looking for adventure .

2. I see _____ flying overhead.

3. It is a gray and _____ day.

4. I worked till midnight, so I am very _____

   today.

5. My sadness _____ heavily on my heart.

6. Memories of his lost love _____ him.

7. My wanderings have _____ that the world is

   indeed round.

COMPREHENSION QUESTIONS

1. In a sentence or two, summarize the main point of the poem.

2. Who is speaking in the poem? Where is he and what is he doing?

3. How long ago was the relationship he is speaking about?

4. What is he feeling and what does he wonder about this old relationship? (What specific words does he use to describe his feelings?)

5. Who ended the relationship, and what are your thoughts about why they separated?

6. What do the last lines mean? "Now if we'd stayed together, / There's much we'd never've known—/ But dreary books and weary lands/ Weigh on me like a stone."

7. Can you find a simile in the poem? (What makes it a simile, rather than a metaphor?)

TOPICS FOR DISCUSSION OR WRITING

1. Have you ever wondered what happened to someone you were close to, but who is no longer in your life? Write about what was special about the relationship, why it ended, and what you regret or wonder about now. If you'd like, try writing down some of these thoughts in the form of a poem.

2. Interview an adult about his or her first love or an early relationship that was very special. What made it so special? Has this person ever had regrets about that relationship? Does he or she know how the other person's life turned out? (You could also make up a story or poem about an older person who remembers back to his or her first love.)

SECTION 2

PREREADING

Write a real (or imaginary) letter to someone whom
you have hurt at some time in your life—perhaps by
words you said when you were hurt or angry. Tell him
or her how you feel about what you said.

Sometimes we do not think about the effect that our words have upon
other people. Our words may hurt someone unintentionally. At other
times we may say hurtful things in order to "get back at" someone or
take revenge on someone who has hurt us. We can even anger or hurt
someone by being silent. Phyllis McGinley's short poem sums up some of
the ways we hurt others.

A CHOICE OF WEAPONS
Phyllis McGinley

Sticks and stones are hard on bone.
Aimed with angry art,
Words can sting like anything.
Silence breaks the heart.

COMPREHENSION QUESTIONS

1. In what way are sticks and stones like angry words?

2. Which part of a person can you hurt with words?

3. How can silence be painful?

4. For whom is the silence painful?

5. What do you think the title, "A Choice of Weapons," means?

6. Is the narrator suggesting that we should say what we feel or be silent—or is she saying something else?

TOPICS FOR DISCUSSION OR WRITING

1. What are some of the ways that your words have hurt other people? Think of a situation when you said something that unintentionally hurt someone. Also think about a time when you *deliberately* said something to hurt another person, perhaps because you were angry with that person, or that person said something that hurt you. Write about one of these experiences.

2. Take the situation that you just wrote about and think of a better way to have handled it. Share your thoughts with a classmate or friend. Ask if this person might have handled the situation differently.

3. Do you recall this phrase from the poem "Who Am I?" (Unit 1): ". . . all the terminology we use to kill each other!"? Can you relate this line to the ideas conveyed in "A Choice of Weapons"?

SECTION 3

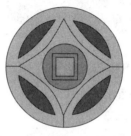

PREREADING

Write a short note to one of your parents, older relative, or caretaker. Explain to him or her why you did something when you were younger that they disapproved of, such as stay out late or smoke a cigarette. You may want to share your ideas with a classmate, your teacher, or the whole class. If you prefer, write your answer in your private journal.

Our relationships with our parents (or adults who care for us) are usually very complicated and influence other relationships throughout our lives. In the next reading, which is an excerpt from Amy Tan's book *The Joy Luck Club*, the relationship between a mother and daughter is revealed through their conversation and their thoughts. Although their relationship is a close one, each feels misunderstood in some ways. As you read the story, think about similar feelings you might have had as a son or daughter, or as a parent.

As you read the selection, be alert to a shift in the point of view of the story—a change in who is speaking. It begins with the daughter speaking about her relationship with her mother, then her mother becomes the speaker and tells her side of the story.

THE JOY LUCK CLUB
Excerpt
Amy Tan

I had taken my mother out to lunch at my favorite Chinese restaurant in hopes of putting her in a good mood, but it was a disaster.

When we met at the Four Directions Restaurant, she eyed me
5 with immediate disapproval. "*Ai-ya!* What's the matter with
your hair?" She said in Chinese.

"What do you mean, 'What's the matter?'" I said. "I had it cut."
Mr. Rory had styled it differently this time, an asymmetrical
blunt-line fringe that was shorter on the left side. It was
10 fashionable, yet not radically so. "Looks chopped off," she said.
"You must ask for your money back."

▼ ▼ ▼

After our miserable lunch, I gave up the idea that there
would ever be a good time to tell her the news: that Rich Shields
and I were getting married.
15 "Why are you so nervous?" my friend Marlene Ferber had
asked over the phone the other night. "It's not as if Rich is the
scum of the earth. He's a tax attorney like you, for Chrissake.
How can she criticize that?"

"You don't know my mother," I said. "She never thinks
20 anybody is good enough for anything."

"So elope with the guy," said Marlene.

"That's what I did with Marvin." Marvin was my first husband,
my high school sweetheart.

"So there you go," said Marlene.
25 "So when my mother found out, she threw her shoe at us," I
said. "And that was just for openers."

▼ ▼ ▼

My mother had never met Rich. In fact every time I brought
up his name—when I said, for instance, that Rich and I had
gone to the symphony, that Rich had taken my four-year-old
30 daughter, Shoshana, to the zoo—my mother found a way to
change the subject.

▼ ▼ ▼

My daughter is getting married a second time. So she asked
me to go to her beauty parlor, her famous Mr. Rory. I know her
meaning. She is ashamed of my looks. What will her husband's
35 parents and his important lawyer friends think of this backward
old Chinese woman?

"Auntie An-mei can cut me," I say.

"Rory is famous," says my daughter, as if she had no ears. "He
does fabulous work."

40 So I sit in Mr. Rory's chair. He pumps me up and down until I am the right height. Then my daughter criticizes me as if I were not there. "See how it's flat on one side," she accuses my head. "She needs a cut and a perm. And this purple tint in her hair, she's been doing it at home. She's never had anything **45** professionally done."

She is looking at Mr. Rory in the mirror. He is looking at me in the mirror. I have seen this professional look before. Americans don't really look at one another when talking. They talk at their reflections. They look at others or themselves only when they **50** think nobody is watching. So they never see how they really

look. They see themselves smiling without their mouths open, or turned to the side where they cannot see their faults. "How does she want it?" asked Mr. Rory. He thinks I do not understand English. He is floating his fingers through my hair. He is showing **55** how his magic can make my hair thicker and longer.

"Ma, how do you want it?" Why does my daughter think she is translating English for me? Before I can even speak, she explains my thoughts: "She wants a soft wave. We probably shouldn't cut it too short. Otherwise it'll be too tight for the **60** wedding. She doesn't want it to look too kinky or weird."

And now she says to me in a loud voice, as if I had lost my hearing, "Isn't that right, Ma? Not too tight?"

I smile. I use my American face. That's the face Americans think is Chinese, the one they cannot understand. But inside I am becoming ashamed. I am ashamed she is ashamed. Because she is my daughter and I am proud of her, and I am her mother and she is not proud of me.

Mr. Rory pats my hair more. He looks at me. He looks at my daughter. Then he says something to my daughter that really displeases her: "It's uncanny how much you two look alike!"

I smile, this time with my Chinese face. But my daughter's eyes and her smile become very narrow, the way a cat pulls itself small just before it bites. Now Mr. Rory goes away so we can think about this. I hear him snap his fingers, "Wash! Mrs. Jong is next!"

So my daughter and I are alone in this crowded beauty parlor. She is frowning at herself in the mirror. She sees me looking at her.

"The same cheeks," she says. She points to mine and then pokes her cheeks. She sucks them outside in to look like a starved person. She puts her face next to mine, side by side, and we look at each other in the mirror.

"You can see your character in your face," I say to my daughter without thinking. "You can see your future."

"What do you mean?" she says.

And now I have to fight back my feelings. These two faces, I think so much the same! The same happiness, the same sadness, the same good fortune, the same faults.

I am seeing myself and my mother, back in China, when I was a young girl.

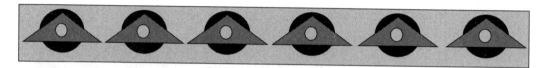

VOCABULARY EXERCISE

Change the part of speech of the word (as needed) at the beginning of the sentence to fit into the sentence correctly.

hope
(line 02)

1. The daughter was _____ about the possibility that she and her mother could communicate better.

different
(line 08)

2. Mr. Rory had styled her hair _____.

disapprove
(line 05)

3. Her mother looked at her with _____.

criticize
(line 18)

4. She did not want to hear any _____ from her mother.

style
(line 08)

5. Her mother did not want a _____ haircut by the famous Mr. Rory.

displease
(line 70)

6. Mr. Rory _____ the daughter when he said that she and her mother resembled each other.

put
(line 81)

7. The daughter _____ her face beside her mother's to compare them.

ashamed
(line 34)

8. The mother thinks the daughter is _____ of her.

pride
(line 66)

9. The mother, on the other hand, is _____ of her daughter.

look
(line 68)

10. The mother _____ at the two of them in the mirror and saw how much they had in common.

COMPREHENSION EXERCISE

Circle TRUE or FALSE depending upon whether each sentence is a true or false statement according to the story. Rewrite the false sentences so that they are true.

TRUE	FALSE	**1.** The daughter works in the Four Directions Restaurant.
TRUE	FALSE	**2.** The daughter is getting married for the second time.
TRUE	FALSE	**3.** When the mother met Richard, they did not get along very well.
TRUE	FALSE	**4.** The mother thinks her daughter is taking her to the beauty parlor because she is ashamed of her.
TRUE	FALSE	**5.** The daughter's husband-to-be is a tax attorney.
TRUE	FALSE	**6.** After talking over their feelings, the mother and daughter have a nice lunch after all.
TRUE	FALSE	**7.** The mother speaks very little English.
TRUE	FALSE	**8.** Mr. Rory thinks the mother and daughter look alike.

COMPREHENSION QUESTIONS

1. What do you know about the daughter's life from the story? For example, what is her marital status? Does she have children? What is her profession?

2. What news does she want to tell her mother at lunch?

3. Why does she say that lunch was "a disaster"?

4. Why does the mother think that the daughter wants to take her to the beauty parlor?

5. Why does the mother say that Mr. Rory doesn't think she speaks English? (What would lead him to think this?)

6. What does the mother mean when she says, "I smile. I use my American face"?

7. How does the mother actually feel about her daughter? Do you think the daughter realizes this? Why or why not? Support your comments with examples from the story.

8. How do you think the daughter feels about her mother? What references in the story lead you to think this?

9. The mother thinks she will be perceived as "a backward old Chinese woman" at the wedding. Do you see her this way? Why or why not? Support your answers with lines from the story.

10. How do some of the incidents in the story illustrate the lines from the McGinley poem "A Choice of Weapons" in Section 2? What are some examples of "words that sting" and the use of silence in the mother and daughter's relationship?

TOPICS FOR DISCUSSION OR WRITING

1. When you read the story, did you find yourself "taking sides"— identifying more with the mother or the daughter? If so, which one and why? (Take a vote in the class to see how many people identify more with the mother versus with the daughter.)

2. Do you think the difficulties in this mother-daughter relationship can be attributed to: (a) cultural differences; (b) generational differences (between an older and a younger person); (c) problems specific to a parent-child relationship?; (d) a combination of factors?

3. Have you ever set out to do something special for someone and have the experience turn out differently than you planned— perhaps it turned into a disaster? Write about this experience—what you had hoped would happen and how it turned out.

4. Think back to a misunderstanding you might have had with your parents (or an adult who took care of you). Write two different versions of the situation. Describe it from both points of view. Write it first from your point of view and include your feelings, words, and actions. Then rewrite it from the other person's point of view, including his or her feelings, words, and actions.

5. Which parent do you resemble the most? Do you also have some personality traits in common with this parent (or caretaker)? Write about these physical and psychological similarities. Also write about whether this is the parent that you are particularly close to or have a difficult relationship with.

6. Write about an old photograph of you with your family or friends. What's going on in the picture? Where does it take place? What do you think the various people in the photograph are feeling? (You may also turn this into an even more imaginative exercise by making up a story about someone else's family snapshot.)

WRITING STRATEGY LESSON: POINT OF VIEW

In order to understand a story or poem, it is important to get a sense of who is talking—to identify the point of view from which it is told. Unless the piece of writing is an essay or autobiography, the author is *not* the same as the narrator or speaker. Therefore, when referring to a character in a story, do not refer to him or her as the author or writer. It is a mistake, for example, to think of Amy Tan as the daughter in *The Joy Luck Club* excerpt.

There are basically three different points of view that a story can be written from:

▼ *The first person*, in which the character uses the first person pronoun *I* to talk about himself or herself, such as in the "Seaman's Ditty."

▼ *The third person*, where there is no speaker's voice, but the people are described in the third person by someone who is present to their situation. The next two stories include some first person plural—"we"—references, but is essentially told from the point of view of a third person.

▼ *An omniscient point of view* (pronounced OM-NI′-SHUNT), where the story is told by a narrator who is omniscient—all-knowing, but invisible to the reader. The narrator is privy to the thoughts and feelings of characters, as well as events throughout their lives. The poem "A Choice of Weapons" is told from an invisible, omniscient point of view.

What is the point of view of these earlier readings? Check back to see, if you are unsure.

From Unit 1: "My Name" _____.

"No One Else" _____.

"Girl" _____.

From Unit 2: "Goldfields Hotel" _____.

"Boricua" _____.

"A Day's Wait" _____.

"Chinatown Talking Story" _____.

From Unit 3: In *The Joy Luck Club*, where does the point of view shift from the daughter in first person to the mother in first person? Note the paragraph numbers: _____.

SECTION 4 A

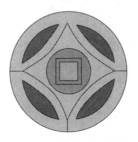

PREREADING

Choose one of these three topics about punishment and write about it for a few minutes.

▼ Were you punished as a child? What did you do? How were you punished? Do you believe the punishment was justified and fair?

▼ If you are a parent yourself, do you punish your children? If so, how do you punish them? How do you feel about this?

▼ What kinds of behaviors should children be punished for? What kinds of punishment are inappropriate for children? When does punishment become child abuse?

You may want to share your ideas with a classmate, your teacher, or the whole class. If you prefer, write your answer in your private journal.

The two readings in this section, "What Sally Said" and "Linoleum Roses," are chapters from *The House on Mango Street* by Sandra Cisneros. After reading both of them, you will see an example of how patterns established in childhood relationships sometimes carry over into adult relationships. Aspects of our childhood, such as how we were treated, the role we played in the family, and how we felt about ourselves are often "re-enacted" in future relationships.

WHAT SALLY SAID
Sandra Cisneros

He never hits me hard. She said her mama rubs lard on the the places where it hurts. Then at school she says she fell. That's where all the blue places come from. That's why her skin is always scarred.

5   But who believes her. A girl that big, a girl who comes in with her pretty face all beaten and black can't be falling off the stairs. He never hits me hard.

But Sally doesn't tell about that time he hit her with his hands just like a dog, she said, like if I was an animal. He thinks I'm
10 going to run away like his sisters who made the family ashamed. Just because I'm a daughter, and then she doesn't say anything else.

Sally was going to get permission to stay with us a little and one Thursday she finally came with a sack full of clothes and a
15 paper bag of sweetbread her mama sent. And would've stayed too except when the dark came her father, whose eyes were little from crying, knocked on the door and said please come back, this is the last time. And she said Daddy and went home.

Then we didn't need to worry. Until one day Sally's father
20 catches her talking to a boy and the next day she doesn't come to school. And the next. Until the way Sally tells it, he just went crazy, he just forgot he was her father between the buckle and the belt.

You're not my daughter, you're not my daughter. And then
25 he broke into his hands.

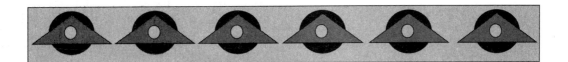

VOCABULARY EXERCISE

Write the word from the list below that best fits in the blank in each sentence. You may have to change the form of the word.

scar	(line 04)	belt	(line 23)
ashamed	(line 11)	worried	(line 19)
permission	(line 13)	buckle	(line 22)

1. Sally's family felt _____ that her sisters had

   run away from home.

2. Sally needed _____ from her father to stay

   with her friend.

3. When her friends saw how sorry Sally's father was about hurting

   her, they didn't _____ anymore.

4. Sometimes Sally's father hit her with a _____

   that had a _____ on it.

5. Sally's body is _____ from being hit so much.

COMPREHENSION QUESTIONS

1. In the first sentence in the story, "He never hits me hard," who is speaking and who is being referred to?

2. When she goes to school, what does Sally say is the reason that she has bruises on her body?

3. Why does Sally's father hit her?

4. Why does Sally go back home and not stay over at her friend's (the narrator's) house?

5. What happened in the last sentence: "And then he broke into his hands"?

WRITING STRATEGY ACTIVITY

The story "What Sally Said" switches point of view a number of times in the story, even in the same paragraph. Go back through the story and circle the pronouns, for example, *I, she, he,* and *we* each time you come upon them. Then make a note next to it identifying who is talking. Is it the narrator? The narrator and Sally's classmates? Sally? Sally's father?

TOPICS FOR DISCUSSION OR WRITING

1. How do you think Sally sees her situation? How does she feel about herself and her father? Imagine that you are Sally and you are keeping a private journal and that you have just had a bad scene with your father. What would you write in your journal?

2. We do not know much about the father from the story except that he punishes Sally because he is afraid that she will do something to shame the family. Imagine that you are the author and that you are going to write a chapter about the father. Shift to his point of view. What name would you give him? What does he look like? What work does he do? How does he spend his time? What are his favorite things to do, to eat, etc.? One approach might be to describe a typical day in the life of the father and incorporate some of this information into your description. Try to capture the essence of this person with a few well-chosen, concrete descriptions.

SECTION 4 B

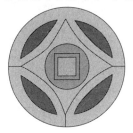

LINOLEUM ROSES
Sandra Cisneros

Sally got married like we knew she would, young and not ready but married just the same. She met a marshmallow salesman at a school bazaar and she married him in another state where it's legal to get married before eighth grade. She
5 has her husband and her house now, her pillowcases and her plates. She says she is in love, but I think she did it to escape.

Sally says she likes being married because now she gets to buy her own things when her husband gives her money. She is happy except sometimes her husband gets angry and once he
10 broke the door where his foot went through, though most days he is okay. Except he won't let her talk on the telephone. And he doesn't like her friends, so nobody gets to visit her unless he is working.

15   She sits at home because she is afraid to go outside without his permission. She looks at all the things they own: the towels and the toaster, the alarm clock and the drapes. She likes looking at the walls, at how neatly their corners meet, the linoleum roses on the floor, the ceiling smooth as wedding cake.

"Linoleum Roses" by Sandra Cisneros from THE HOUSE ON MANGO STREET. Copyright © 1989 by Sandra Cisneros. Published in the United States by Vintage Books, a division of Random House, Inc., New York. Reprinted by permission of Susan Bergholz Literary Services, New York.

COMPREHENSION EXERCISE

Choose the statement that correctly completes each sentence.

1. Sally married . . .

_____ **a.** before she reached the eighth grade in school.

_____ **b.** when she reached the age of 16.

_____ **c.** with her father's permission.

_____ **d.** because she was tired of going to school.

2. The man Sally married . . .

_____ **a.** lived in another state.

_____ **b.** was a shoe salesman.

_____ **c.** was a marshmallow salesman.

_____ **d.** is much nicer than her father was.

3. Sally likes being married because . . .

_____ **a.** her husband loves her very much.

_____ **b.** she can buy her own things.

_____ **c.** she doesn't have to go to school.

_____ **d.** she always gets to talk to her friends on the telephone.

COMPREHENSION QUESTIONS

1. Who is Sally's husband?

2. Why did she get married?

3. What does she like about being married?

4. How does her husband treat her? What does he not let her do? Why do you think he treats her like this?

5. What does she do all day?

6. Why do you think the story is called "Linoleum Roses"?

WRITING STRATEGY ACTIVITIES

1. Who is the narrator of the story—from whose point of view is it told?
2. Find at least three examples of the author's use of specific, concrete language to convey to the reader a sense of Sally's world.

TOPICS FOR DISCUSSION OR WRITING

1. Do you think Sally's husband will ever hit her like her father did? Since he does have a tendency to violence like her father, write about why you think she married a man who may end up treating her like her father did.
2. Imagine that Sally is your friend, write her a letter telling her how you feel about her situation and how might she handle it.
3. Along one side of a sheet of paper, make a list of adjectives that describe you best, such as *shy, kind, easily angered, messy, athletic,* etc. Along the other side of the page, list words that describe how you want your ideal partner to be. (If you are already married or involved with someone, this assignment could be even more interesting if you make a third column down the page that lists his or her actual characteristics. Then compare the three lists.) After completing this exercise, the class could compare and discuss their lists of ideal characteristics in a partner.
4. Bring to class an example of a personal advertisement from the classified section of a newspaper, in which someone is looking for a relationship. Write your own personal ad, describing yourself and what you're looking for in a partner. (You don't have to actually send it to a newspaper!)

UNIT 4 CHANGES

The theme of of this unit is CHANGES. A person goes through many changes in life. The first reading selection in the unit, from Ecclesiastes in the *Bible*, tells us that there is a time and a reason for everything that happens to us. Do you agree with this? If you had to choose the two or three most important changes in your life, what would they be? Sometimes the changes we experience are public, such as getting married or moving to a new country. But some of the most important changes are ones that take place inside of us—changes that affect how we see ourselves and experience what life has to offer. As with the other units, the selections here will take you into the thoughts and feelings of people as they experience change. In each situation, think about how you would react to the same experience.

SECTION 1

PREREADING

Before reading the verse, take a few minutes and write about an experience that changed your life. Explain whether it was for the better or not. You may want to share your ideas with a classmate, your teacher, or the whole class. If you prefer, write your answer in your private journal.

A saying that one hears sometimes is "timing is everything." Comedians talk about timing being critical in telling a joke. If the timing is off, the joke won't be as funny. In the poem by Gary Snyder in Unit 3, the seaman wonders about an old love. If they had met at a different time in life, do you think that they might have gotten together? Do you ever wonder about experiences in your life being different if they had happened at a different time? The next selection is a verse from Ecclesiastes. According to the verse, everything has a right time to happen and a "purpose under the heaven."

ECCLESIASTES
Chapter 3, Verses 1 to 8

To everything there is a season,
And a time to every purpose under the heaven:
A time to be born, and a time to die;
A time to plant, and a time to pluck up that which is planted;
5   A time to kill, and a time to heal;
A time to break down, and a time to build up;
A time to weep, and a time to laugh;
A time to mourn, and a time to dance;
A time to cast away stones, and a time to gather stones
10   together;
A time to embrace, and a time to refrain from embracing;
A time to get, and a time to lose;
A time to keep, and a time to cast away;
A time to rend, and a time to sew;
15   A time to keep silence, and a time to speak;
A time to love, and a time to hate;
A time of war, and a time of peace.

Ecclesiastes is reprinted from the Old Testament in THE HOLY BIBLE, King James Version; Chapter 3, Verses 1 to 8.

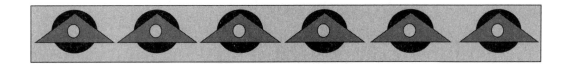

VOCABULARY EXERCISE

Without looking back at the verse, try to match the words at the left with their opposites in the list on the right.

love	cast away
keep silence	die
keep	peace
get	build up
born	hate
war	pluck up
rend	speak
break down	sew
plant	lose

COMPREHENSION QUESTIONS

1. What is the most important word repeated throughout the verse?

2. Why does the speaker use contrasts?

3. What do you think the poem is saying about the changes that a person may go through in life?

TOPICS FOR DISCUSSION OR WRITING

1. Do you believe that there is a purpose for everything that happens to you? Or do you think that some things happen without a purpose, accidently or randomly?

2. The speaker says that there is even a right time to break down, to hate, to kill, to make war. Do these lines surprise you? Do you agree or disagree with them?

3. Can you think of an internal change that you see in yourself over the last few years—something no one else might see? Perhaps there is a change in

   ▼ how you see yourself,

   ▼ how you feel about the future, or

   ▼ how you approach a difficult situation or challenge, compared to when you were younger.

4. This selection from Ecclesiastes is very well known. It has even become a popular song. Can you explain why it is so popular? What universal truths does it contain?

WRITING STRATEGY LESSON: TRANSITIONAL TECHNIQUES

This unit is about life changes, thus it seems appropriate to look at how writers make transitions in their writing—how they get from one sentence to another or from one idea to another. There are many different ways to "glue" a story together. Transitional techniques encompass words, paragraphs, and the overall sequence and structure chosen for a piece of writing. In the Ecclesiastes verse, the ideas flow smoothly and rhythmically, almost like music, because of the repetition of a particular phrase. What is that phrase?

What other poems or stories in the units you have read are linked together in this rhythmical way by repetition and parallel phrasing?

The story that follows is told chronologically—that is, in a logical time order. Read the story once for meaning. Then look back over it and circle transitional words that help you understand the sequence of the events.

SECTION 2

PREREADING

The following is a five-minute writing exercise. Make a list of all the thoughts and feelings that come to mind when you consider moving from one country or community to another. Compare your list with a classmate's. Are there some similarities in your lists? What things are different?

The story that follows, excerpted from the novel *The Nowhere Man* by Kamala Markandaya, is about an immigrant and his family. The main character is Srinivas, an Indian who lives in London. His wife, Vasantha, has just died. Their son's name is Laxman. As you read the story, think about whether you identify more with Srinivas or with Vasantha.

THE NOWHERE MAN
Excerpt
Kamala Markandaya

Outside the crematorium chapel a green-coated attendant handed Srinivas the casket. It was very light. Five pounds, or so, of ash.

"It's all done up, guv'," he said. "Sealed, so you won't have no
5 trouble with spillage." He paused, considering, then came out with it. "Now don't you fret yourself," he said kindly. "I mean it comes to us all in the end. If you take my advice you'll scatter the ashes. It don't do any good brooding over them like."

"I shall take your advice," promised Srinivas, and got on a bus
10 with the casket. It was a difficult thing to do, for besides the casket he was carrying Vasantha's sandalwood box which she had filled with earth from India and brought with her, and her hair-oil bottle half full of Ganges water. Laxman should have carried these, but Laxman was in bed with influenza. So he
15 managed, somehow, on his own.

At London Bridge he alighted. There was a catwalk, and steps leading down to the river. The tide was in, there was not far to go: five or six steps, and the sluggish Thames was slopping over his toe-caps. Srinivas put down the box and bottle
20 while he broke the seals on the casket.

Then he opened it gently, and leaning out as far as he could so that they should not be washed back, he tipped the ashes into the river. Afterwards there remained only the small service she had asked of him and this he performed, sprinkling earth
25 and Ganges water onto the ashes being borne away on the Thames.

He was, at that period of his life, beginning to lose the fetters which tied him to any one country. He was a human being, and as such felt he belonged to a wider citizenship. Yet, in this
30 moment, he could not help feeling with Vasantha, who in her breath and bones had remained wholly Indian. She would have liked her remains committed to the currents of an Indian

river, though she had scrupulously refrained from such onerous impositions; and now, watching her ashes drift away
35 downstream, he wished he could have found some way to avoid consigning them to these alien waters. A sauntering policeman, pausing to lean over the parapet, observed the proceedings. He waited for Srinivas to come up and said reprovingly, "You are not allowed to tip your household rubbish
40 into the river."

"I would not dream of doing so," said Srinivas.

"I'm sorry, sir, but you did," accused the policeman. "I saw you. If everyone carried on the same the river would soon be polluted." Here it occurred to him that it already was: a very
45 fine array of floating debris was being shunted gently along by the tide. The constable averted his eyes. "Well, just see you don't do it again," he said, and prepared to move on. "The river's not the place for rubbish."

"It was not rubbish," said Srinivas, and found to his dismay
50 that his throat was working painfully. "It was my wife."

Joker, eh, thought the policeman tersely; but the sharp words died on his lips as he whipped around smartly, because he

could see that the middle-aged Indian before him was weeping. Or was as close to it as any man could be, in the
55 presence of another. The constable reddened, being young and decent as the young often are; then he touched his helmet, awkwardly, to the stricken man, and walked on.

VOCABULARY EXERCISE

Match the words from the story with their definitions. If you need to, look back at the story to find context clues to the meaning of these words. After you have tried to guess the meanings, check your answers in the dictionary.

a. fetters   (line 27)
b. scrupulous   (line 33)
c. onerous   (line 33)
d. sauntering   (line 36)
e. reproving   (line 39)
f. shunted   (line 45)
g. terse   (line 51)

h. scatter   (line 07)
i. sprinkle   (line 24)
j. alien   (line 36)
k. fret   (line 06)
l. brood   (line 08)
m. ashes   (line 08)
n. stricken   (line 57)

_____ heavy, burdensome

_____ critical

_____ brief, to the point

_____ pushed

_____ very careful

_____ ties, chains

_____ walking casually

_____ to scatter in small drops
           or grains

_____ to think sadly about

_____ to separate or distribute
           widely

_____ belonging to another
           country

_____ affected by grief or
           misfortune

_____ the fine dust or powder
           that remains after
           something is burned

_____ to worry or become upset

After you have worked with the previous words, complete the following sentences with the correct words from the list. You might need to change the form of the word to fit the particular sentence.

1. The farmer is rather old-fashioned; he still _____ the seeds by hand.

2. Please go and _____ some water on the path in order to keep the dust down.

3. An American is a/an _____ in Great Britain.

4. The sad old woman lay in her hospital bed _____ about her misfortunes.

5. What are you _____ about? Everything will work out just fine.

6. After the party ended, the children put out the fire and covered the _____ with sand.

7. They were _____ with fear upon seeing the wild animal and could not even move to defend themselves.

8. The animal had _____ on his legs so that he couldn't run away.

9. The cat _____ out of the kitchen after her meal.

10. I have a five-year report to write at work. What a/an _____ task!

COMPREHENSION EXERCISE

Put the following sentences in the order in which they happened in the story by numbering them from 1 to 6. Try not to look back at the story other than to check your answers when you finish.

_____ **a.** Vasantha's ashes are sprinkled over the Thames river.

_____ **b.** A policeman accuses Srinivas of throwing rubbish in the river.

_____ **c.** Srinivas picks up his dead wife's ashes from the crematorium.

_____ **d.** Srinivas carries the casket and a box filled with earth from India to a river in London.

_____ **e.** Srinivas begins to cry when he tells the policeman that the "rubbish" is his wife's ashes.

_____ **f.** The man at the crematorium advises Srinivas not to hold onto the ashes and brood about his wife's death, but to scatter the ashes instead.

COMPREHENSION QUESTIONS

1. Why does Srinivas scatter his wife's ashes on the river?

2. Why is Srinivas's son Laxman not with him when he goes to the river?

3. Where does Srinivas wish he could scatter Vasantha's ashes? Why?

4. What does Srinivas tell us is the difference between how he feels about living in a new country and how his wife felt about it?

5. What does the policeman accuse Srinivas of doing?

6. How does Srinivas react to this accusation?

7. How does the policeman respond to this reaction from Srinivas? Do you think he realizes what Srinivas is doing?

8. What do you think the title *The Nowhere Man* means?

TOPICS FOR DISCUSSION OR WRITING

1. Have you ever felt like a "nowhere man"? Write about these feelings and why you felt this way. You might consider writing a poem on this theme.
2. Why do you think some people adapt well to a new environment and others retain their original cultural identity?
3. Do you identify more with Srinivas or with Vasantha with regard to adaptability to a new culture? Srinivas sees himself as a human being first who "belonged to a wider citizenship," and, therefore, could perhaps live almost anywhere he chose. Vasantha, on the other hand, "remained wholly Indian." Place an **x** on the line below according to whether you (or someone you know) is more like Srinivas or Vasantha—or somewhere in the middle. (This type of line is referred to as a *continuum*, a continuous whole that can't be separated into parts.) Explain your reasons for these perceptions.

SRINIVAS   VASANTHA
(extremely   (strong identification
adaptive)   with the original culture)

4. Retell the story from the point of view of Laxman as an adult as he recollects these experiences from his childhood.
5. Pretend that Srinivas discovers a letter to him from Vasantha to be read after her death. Assume that Vasantha feels free to speak her heart. What might she have written to her husband?

SECTION 3

PREREADING

Make a list of some of the things you might find strange if you went to live in a new country. If you prefer, make a list of the experiences you might find strange if you went back to live in a place where you have lived before. You may want to share your ideas with a classmate, your teacher, or the whole class. Or write your answer in your private journal.

In her short story, the Canadian writer Margaret Laurence describes the problems of an African scientist who has lived in England for many years. When Dr. Quansah returns to live in Africa where he was born, he finds that he doesn't fit in anymore. The narrator of the story, Miss Nedden, has come to Africa from a European country to teach English. She also has problems coping with different cultures. Ruth Quansah, Dr. Quansah's daughter, is one of her pupils. Miss Nedden tries to help Dr. Quansah to deal with his daughter's problems in adjusting to life in Africa. What do you think might happen to you if you returned to live in the country where you were born after living abroad for some time? Could you cope with all the changes?

THE RAIN CHILD
Excerpt
Margaret Laurence

Each Friday Dr. Quansah drove over to see Ruth, and usually on these afternoons he would call in at my bungalow for a few minutes to discuss her progress. At first our conversations were completely false, each of us telling the other that Ruth was
5 getting on reasonably well. Then one day he dropped the pretense.

"She is very unhappy, isn't she? Please—don't think I am blaming you, Miss Nedden. Myself, rather. It is too different. What should I have done, all those years ago?"

10 "Don't be offended, Dr. Quansah, but why wasn't she taught her own language?"

He waited a long moment before replying. He studied the clear amber tea in his cup.

"I was brought up in a small village," he said at last. "English
15 came hard to me. When I went to Secondary School I experienced great difficulty at first in understanding even the gist of the lectures. I was determined that the same thing would not happen to Ruth. I suppose I imagined she would pick up her own language easily, once she returned here, as though the
20 knowledge of one's family tongue was inherited. Of course, if her mother had lived—"

He set down the teacup and knotted his huge hands together in an unexpressed anguish that was painful to see.

"Both of them uprooted," he said. "It was my fault, I guess,
25 and yet—"

He fell silent. Finally, his need to speak was greater than his reluctance to reveal himself.

"You see, my wife hated England, always. I knew, although she never spoke of it. Such women don't. She was a quiet
30 woman, gentle and—obedient. My parents had chosen her and I had married her when I was a very young man, before I first left this country. Our differences were not so great, then, but later in those years in London—she was like a plant, expected to grow where the soil is not suitable for it. My friends and
35 associates—the places I went for dinner—she did not accompany me. I never asked her to entertain those people in our house. I could not—you see that?"

I nodded and he continued in the same low voice with its burden of self-reproach.

40 "She was illiterate," he said. "She did not know anything of my life, as it became. She did not want to know. She refused to learn. I was—impatient with her. I know that. But -"
He turned away so I would not see his face.
"Have you any idea what it is like," he cried, "to need
45 someone to talk to, and not have even one person?"
"Yes," I said. "I have a thorough knowledge of that."
He looked at me in surprise, and when he saw that I did know, he seemed oddly relieved, as though, having exchanged vulnerabilities, we were neither of us endangered.
50 My ebony cane slipped to the ground just then, and Dr. Quansah stooped and picked it up, automatically and casually, hardly noticing it, and I was startled at myself, for I had felt no awkwardness in the moment either.
"When she became ill," he went on, "I do not think she really
55 cared whether she lived or not. And now, Ruth—you know, when she was born, my wife called her an African name which means 'child of the rain'." My wife missed the sun so very much. The rain too, may have stood for her own tears. She had not wanted to bear her child so far from home."
60 Unexpectedly, he smiled, the dark features of his face relaxing, becoming less blunt and plain.
"Why did you leave your country and come here, Miss Nedden? For the church? Or for the sake of the Africans?
I leaned back in my mock throne and re-arranged, a shade
65 ironically, the folds of my lilac smock.
"I thought so, once," I replied. "But now I don't know. I think I may have come here mainly for myself after all, hoping to find a place where my light could shine forth. Not a very palatable admission, perhaps."
70 "At least you did not take others along on your pilgrimage."
"No. I took no one. No one at all."
We sat without speaking, then until the tea grew cold and the dusk gathered.

▼　▼　▼

"I have been away a long time, Miss Nedden," he said, "but
75 not long enough to forget some of the things that were said to me by Europeans when I was young."

I should not have blurted out my immediate thought, but I did.

"You have been able to talk to me—"

80 "Yes." He smiled self-mockingly. "I wonder if you know how much that has surprised me?"

Why should I have found it difficult then, to look at him, at the face whose composure I knew concealed such aloneness. I took refuge, as so often, in the adoption of an abrupt tone.

85 "Why should it be surprising? You liked people in England. You had friends there."

"I am not consistent, I know. But the English at home are not the same as the English abroad—you must have realized that. You are not typical, Miss Nedden, I still find most Europeans

90 here as difficult to deal with as I ever did. And yet—I seem to have lost touch with my own people too. The young laboratory technicians at the station—they do not trust me, and I find myself getting so very impatient with them, losing my temper because they have not comprehended what I wanted them to

95 do, and—"

He broke off. "I really shouldn't bother you with all this."

"Oh, but you're not." The words came out with an unthinking swiftness which mortified me later when I recalled it. "I haven't so many people I can talk with either, you know."

100 "You told me as much, once," Dr. Quansah said gently. "I had not forgotten."

VOCABULARY EXERCISE

Some of the words in this passage may be new to you. Change the form of these words so that they fit into the sentence correctly. This exercise should help you to understand the meaning of the words.

offend

(line 10)

1. The hostess was really _____ when her guest refused to taste the food.

pretend

(line 06)

2. The guest should at least have made a _____ of eating so that the hostess wouldn't be upset.

palate

(line 68)

3. Many children say that they don't find caviar _____.

reluctance

(line 27)

4. My children were _____ to taste new foods.

blurt

(line 77)

5. Once when my daughter was very young, she _____ out that the food she was given at her grandmother's house was disgusting.

compose

(line 83)

6. Today she's grown up and has the _____ to handle difficult situations.

COMPREHENSION QUESTIONS

1. Why did Dr. Quansah leave Africa to go and live in England?

2. Describe the kind of marriage he and his wife had.

3. Why was Mrs. Quansah so unhappy living in England?

4. What does Ruth's African name mean? Why did her mother give her that name?

5. Why didn't Ruth learn her own language?

6. What personal problem do Dr. Quansah and Miss Nedden share?

7. Why did Miss Nedden leave her country and go to live in Africa?

8. Dr. Quansah says that he is not consistent about his attitude to Europeans. Can you explain what he means?

9. What kind of problems does he have with the young laboratory technicians who work for him?

10. Dr. Quansah is suffering from anomie—a lack of identity. He doesn't belong anywhere. Can you quote some of the things he says to prove this?

11. Why do you think this story is called "The Rain Child"?

TOPICS FOR DISCUSSION OR WRITING

1. Which character from an earlier story does Dr. Quansah's wife remind you of? Why?

2. How do you feel about Dr. Quansah's decision not to have his daughter learn her native African language? Do you agree or disagree with this decision? (This question lends itself to an interesting class debate. How many people are on one side of the question? How many are on the other side?)

3. How important is it to you to be able to speak the language of a country that you visit or move to? Is it extremely important? Somewhat important? Or not so important? Explain your response.

4. Imagine that you are Ruth. Write a letter to a friend in England telling her about your new life in Africa.

5. After you have lived in a new country for a number of years, do you think it's possible to "go home again"? Speaking from your own experience or from that of someone you know, what might some of the problems be?

6. Do you think it's easier for men or women to adjust to a new culture? Refer to some of the stories you've read to support or illustrate your point of view. You may also use real life experience to explain your position. (This question, too, would make an interesting class debate.)

7. Dr. Quansah says that English people are different at home in England from the English who live abroad. Do you think that this is possible? Is this true for other groups of people? If you think it is true, give examples of the different kinds of behavior. Can you explain how such a thing could happen?

8. How are you different in different cultures or settings? Complete these phrases about yourself:

a. When I am in my native culture, I am more _____

_____.

b. When I am in a new culture or environment, I am more _____

_____.

c. With my family, I am more _____

_____.

d. With my friends, I am more _____

_____ .

e. With my co-workers or classmates, I am more _____

_____ .

f. With strangers, I am more _____

_____ .

WRITING STRATEGY ACTIVITY

From the list below, choose a transition word that relates the parts of the sentence logically. More than one choice might make sense in some of the sentences.

after	since
if	however
therefore	during
when	while
because	until
before	

1. I don't usually eat meat, _____ I will have a little of that chicken salad for lunch.

2. I don't often get to bed _____ midnight.

3. I sometimes sing _____ I take a shower.

4. The telephone rang _____ my favorite television program.

5. The child is six, _____ she is too young to be home alone.

6. _____ I am finished with my schoolwork, let's go to a movie.

7. _____ it rains, I have to cover the broken car

window.

8. _____ the ball game, let's get some dinner.

9. I haven't had a pizza _____ Maria and Carlos

come to dinner a few weeks ago.

10. _____ you help me with the laundry, I'll help

you organize the study.

SECTION 4

PREREADING

If you had to leave your home and country suddenly and could only take five things with you, what would they be? Take a few minutes and write down what you would take. Share your list with a classmate. Perhaps you or someone in the class has actually faced a similar dilemma. Have them recount their experience.

The poem "Okasan/Mother" by Sakae S. Roberson, also deals with adapting to a new culture and the changes that this type of experience brings about in one's life. We get a glimpse of how another person has experienced this kind of "uprooting." Keep in mind *The Nowhere Man* as you read this poem. In what ways is "Okasan/Mother" similar to or different than the people we met in the previous readings?

OKASAN / MOTHER
Sakae S. Roberson

twenty-five years she's been here
and still
   a-me-ri-ka makes her mouth sour tight
   sticks in her mind like spit-wet thread
5   caught in the eye of a needle.

twenty-five years of doing christmas
and still
   she saves generation-old
bamboo mats for wrapping new year osushi/
10   rice cakes
   hums songs of japan
in the quiet dark of christmas mornings.

every year
for twenty-five years she plans new year

15　every year
for twenty-five years she plans new year
and still
　　one more dress to sew. one more bill to pay.
　　one more year passes.
20　　she celebrates
sewing silk gowns for rich ladies.

twenty-five years
　　and still
　　she tells no stories of war to a daughter
25　　she saves marriage lace and
　　satin baby kimonos in a cedar chest for
　　a daughter who denies her conversation
　　　watches her sew her life designs
　　into someone else's wedding day

30　twenty-five years of city living
people calling her oriental or chinese
sometimes jap
　　and still
　　her eyes, like teardrops turned sideways,
35　　say nothing.
　　with pride, she writes from right to left
　　of the greatness of a-me-ri-ka to her people.

twenty-five years
　　alone.
40　　still
she cries in japanese.

COMPREHENSION EXERCISE

After you have read the poem, circle TRUE or FALSE next to the sentences below. After you have completed them, go back and find lines in the poem which support your true or false answers. Revise any false statements to make them true.

TRUE	FALSE	**1.** Okasan/Mother has lived in America for twenty-five years.
TRUE	FALSE	**2.** She wishes that her daughter were more interested in Japanese culture.
TRUE	FALSE	**3.** She is sewing a wedding dress for her daughter.
TRUE	FALSE	**4.** She celebrates Christmas (even though the holiday is not part of the traditional religion in Japan).
TRUE	FALSE	**5.** She and her daughter have a close relationship.
TRUE	FALSE	**6.** Americans sometimes mistake Okasan/Mother for Chinese.
TRUE	FALSE	**7.** She hopes her daughter will have a baby.

COMPREHENSION QUESTIONS

1. What does Okasan/Mother do for a living?

2. What are some of the things that she does which reveal that she still feels closely tied to Japan?

3. What are some of the ways she has adapted to living in America?

4. What evidence do you have that she feels some gratitude toward America?

5. What lines in the poem illustrate how Americans have treated her?

6. Whom do you think Okasan/Mother is most similar to: Srinivas or Vasantha (in *The Nowhere Man*), Dr. Quansah or his wife (in "The Rain Child")?

WRITING STRATEGY ACTIVITIES

1. It was mentioned earlier that repeated, parallel phrases in the Ecclesiastes verse help establish its rhythm and transitions. There is also a repeated phrase in "Okasan/Mother." Can you find it? Why do you think it is repeated so frequently—what meaning or emphasis does it add to the poem? Are there other repetitious words or phrases in the poem?

2. The writer uses specific, concrete words in the poem to evoke the character and life experience of Okasan/Mother. Circle words in the poem that are particularly descriptive and evocative.

3. There are two examples of similes in "Okasan/Mother" where the author makes a comparison that includes the word *like* in order to make her description more vivid. Can you find these two examples? Write the line and its number here:

Line number: _____

_____.

Line number: _____

_____.

TOPICS FOR DISCUSSION OR WRITING

1. Compare the mother-daughter relationship in the reading from *The Joy Luck Club* (Unit 3), with the relationship described in "Okasan/Mother."

2. Complete the following sentences with your own thoughts about the United States. If you are a native American, you may respond to the questions or answer them in relation to another group of people or a locale where you have lived or visited.

a. In the United States, a person is expected to _____

_____.

b. One trait I like about Americans is _____

_____.

c. A trait I especially dislike about Americans is _____

_____.

d. One surprise I had when I moved to the United States (or moved to

_____) was _____.

e. One thing I'd like to change about living in the United States is

_____

_____.

3. Interview a classmate or acquaintance who is an immigrant and explore how comfortable or uncomfortable this person feels in his or her new environment. Does the person consider that he or she has adapted well to the new home, or would the person prefer to be back in the country of origin? What is missed most and least about his or her former home? Does the person see any differences in his or her personality here, compared to his or her personality before?

SECTION 5

PREREADING

If you suddenly became rich overnight, what would you change about your life? Take a few minutes to write what you would do. You may want to share your ideas with a classmate, your teacher, or the whole class. If you prefer, write your answer in your private journal.

The next story is from an autobiography by Moss Hart, an American playwright, whose family had emigrated from Eastern Europe. Moss Hart was a first–generation American. This excerpt from his book *Act One* tells about the change in his life that came about as a result of the success of his first hit play on Broadway. His play *Once in a Lifetime*, co–written with George S. Kaufman, was an instant hit. This part of the story begins with his journey home the night after his first great success. As you read the story, think about what you would do if you were suddenly rich and famous! Would you do the same thing Moss Hart did?

ACT ONE
Excerpt

Moss Hart

Can success change the human mechanism so completely between one dawn and another? Can it make one feel taller, more alive, handsomer, uncommonly gifted and indomitably secure with the certainty that this is the way life will always be?
5   It can and it does! . . . A cab pulled up beside us and Joe Hyman and I silently shook hands. The driver eyed me warily when I gave him a Brooklyn address, and I was conscious, looking at Joe Hyman, of how disreputable I too must look. I looked at him again and burst into laughter. His eyes were red-
10   rimmed with excitement and weariness, his face grimy with a

full day-and-night's growth of beard, and his suit looked as though he had slept in it. The driver obviously and quite rightly was wondering if there was enough money between us to pay for that long ride, or if we had not already spent every cent in
15   some speakeasy. I took a ten-dollar bill out of my pocket and waved it at him and climbed into the cab. I waved at Joe

Hyman through the rear window until the cab turned the corner, and then settled back in the seat, determined that I would not fall asleep. I had no intention of dozing through the
20 first ride to Brooklyn above ground—I intended to enjoy every visible moment of it and I very shortly reaped the reward for staying awake.

▼ ▼ ▼

No one has ever seen the skyline of the city from Brooklyn Bridge as I saw it that morning with three hit notices under my
25 arm. The face of the city is always invested with grandeur, but grandeur can be chilling. The overpowering symmetry of that skyline can crush the spirit and make the city seem forbidding and impenetrable, but today it seemed to emerge from cold anonymity and grant its acknowledgement and acceptance.
30 There was no sunlight—it was a gray day and the buildings were half shrouded in mist, but it was a city that would know my name today, a city that had not turned me aside, a city that I loved. Unexpectedly, and without warning, a great wave of feeling for this proud and beautiful city swept over me. We
35 were off the bridge now and driving through the sprawling, ugly area of tenements that stretch intermittently over the approaches to each of its boroughs. They are the first in the city to awake, and the long unending rows of drab, identical houses were already stirring with life. Laundry was being strung out to
40 dry along roof tops and fire escapes, men with lunch boxes were coming out of the houses, and children returning from the corner grocery with bottles of milk and loaves of bread were hurrying up the steps and into the doorways.
    I stared through the taxi window at a pinch-faced ten-year-
45 old hurrying down the steps on some morning errand before school, and I thought of myself hurrying down the street on so many gray mornings out a doorway and a house much the same as this one. My mind jumped backward in time and then whirled forward, like a many-faceted prism—flashing our old
50 neighborhood in front of me, the house, the steps, the candy store—and then shifted to the skyline I had just passed by, the opening last night, and the notices I still hugged tightly under my arm. It was possible in this wonderful city for that nameless little boy—for any of its millions—to have a decent chance to
55 scale the walls and achieve what they wished. Wealth, rank or an imposing name counted for nothing. The only credential the city asked was the boldness to dream. For those who did, it

unlocked its gates and its treasures, not caring who they were
or where they came from. I watched the boy disappear into a
60 tailor's shop, and a surge of shamefaced patriotism
overwhelmed me. I might have been watching a victory
parade on a flag-draped Fifth Avenue instead of the mean
streets of a city slum. A feeling of patriotism, however, is not
always limited to the feverish emotions called forth by war. It
65 can sometimes be felt as profoundly and perhaps more truly at
a moment such as this.
    It had suddenly begun to rain very hard, and in a few
minutes I could no longer see much of anything through the
windows. All too quickly I made that swift turnabout from
70 patriotism to enlightened self-interest. I closed my eyes and
thought about how I would spend the money that would soon
start to pour in. To my surprise, affluence did not seem nearly as
easy to settle into as I had always imagined it would be. Try as I
would, I could not think of how to begin or in what ways I
75 wanted to spend the large sums that would now be mine to
command. I could think of little ways to spend it—new suits,
new shirts, new ties, new overcoats—but after that my mind
went disappointingly blank. In some ways sudden riches are
easier to live with than poverty. Both demand artistry of a kind,
80 if one or the other is not to leave the mark of a sour and
lingering cynicism, and opulence in many ways is harder to
manage than penury. It is, however, one of the pleasantest
problems with which to to drift off to sleep. I cheated myself out
of the major portion of the first taxi ride by sleeping soundly
85 through the rest of it. The driver had to leave his seat and shake
me awake to collect his fare.
    I was wide awake again, thoroughly wide awake, and
disappointed to find the shades still drawn and the family fast
asleep when I unlocked the door and stepped into the
90 apartment. It was, of course, only a little after seven o'clock in
the morning, but today was too memorable a day to waste on
anything so commonplace as sleep. I was tempted to wake
them up at once and show them the other notices, but I went
into the kitchen instead and fixed a pot of coffee. I wanted a
95 little more time alone to think about something.
    I stood in the doorway of the kitchen while I waited for the
water to boil and gazed at the sleeping figure of my brother on
the daybed in the dining-room, and beyond it at the closed
door of the one bedroom where my parents slept. The frayed
100 carpet on the floor was the carpet I had crawled over before I

could walk. Each flower in the badly faded and worn design was sharply etched in my mind. Each piece of furniture in the cramped dim room seemed mildewed with a thousand leaden meals hovered over the dining-room table. The dust of countless
105 black-hearted days clung to every crevice of the squalid ugly furniture I had known since childhood. To walk out of it forever—not piecemeal, but completely—would give meaning to the wonder of what had happened to me, make success tangible, decisive.
110 The goal behind the struggle for success is not always one goal, but many—some real, some hidden; some impossible to achieve, even with success piled upon success. The goal differs with each of us in the mysterious and wonderful way each human being is different from any other, in the way each of us
115 is the sum total of the unexpressed longings and desires that strew the seas of childhood and are glimpsed long afterward from a safe distance—a submerged iceberg, only the tip of which is seen.

Whatever dominant force in my nature shaped the blind
120 demands that made it imperative to me to make the theater my goal had taken possession of me early, and I was still possessed by it. What fulfillment it held I would know only when I walked resolutely out of one world and into another. I poured myself a cup of coffee, and by the time I had finished it, my mind was
125 made up.

It is always best if one is about to embark on a wild or reckless venture not to discuss it with anybody beforehand. Talk will rob the scheme of its fire and make what seemed mettlesome and daring merely foolhardy. It is easier on
130 everyone concerned to present it as an accomplished fact, turn a deaf ear to argument, and go ahead with it.

I awakened my brother by dumping the papers on the bed for him to read and then called through the bedroom door to my mother and father to get up right away. I gave them barely
135 enough time to read the notices and then plunged. "We're moving into New York today—as soon as you have a cup of coffee—and we're not taking anything with us. We're walking out of here with just the clothes on our backs and nothing else. The coffee's on the stove, so hurry up and get dressed."
140 My mother stared at me and then spoke quietly, as if a raised voice at this moment might send me further out of my senses. "Where are we going?" she asked logically enough.

"To a hotel," I said, "until we find an apartment and furnish it."
There was a stunned silence and before anyone else could
145   speak, I spoke again, not impatiently but as if what I was
saying was unarguable. "There's nothing to pack; we just walk
out of the door. No," I added in answer to my mother's mute
startled look around the room, "not a thing. We leave it all here
just as it stands, and close the door. We don't take anything—
150   not even a toothbrush, a bathrobe, pajamas, or nightgown. We
buy it all new in New York. We're walking out of here and
starting fresh."

My mother walked to the window and pulled up the shades
as though she might hear or understand what I was saying
155   better with more light, and then turned helplessly toward my
father.

    He was the first to recover his breath and his wits. "We just
paid two months' rent in advance," he said as though that solid
fact would help me recover my own.

160   "That gives us the right to let this stuff sit here and rot, or you
can give it to the janitor," I replied. "We're walking out of here
with just what clothes you put on, and tomorrow we'll get rid of
those, too."

This second bit of information created an even more
165 astonished silence than the first. "Don't you understand?" I heard
myself shouting. "All I'm asking you to do now is—"

"I'm not walking out of here without the pictures," my mother
said with great firmness.

It was my turn to be astonished. "What pictures?" I asked.
170 "All the pictures," she replied. "The baby pictures of you and
Bernie and the pictures of my father and my sister, and Bernie's
diploma and your letters, and all the other pictures and things
I've got in the closet in that big box."

I threw my arms around her and kissed her. I had won. It was
175 being accepted as a fact—incomprehensible but settled.

"One suitcase," I ordered. "Put it all into one suitcase, but one
suitcase—that's all."

I looked at my brother, who had remained silent through all
of this. He handed the papers back to me with a flourish and
180 winked. "Don't you have to give some of the money to George
Kaufman?" he said.

"Half," I replied. "But my share will be over a thousand dollars
a week."

"That'll buy a lot of toothbrushes," he said. "I'm going to get
185 ready." And he climbed out of bed.

My mother and father stared at us as if to make sure we were
not indulging in some elaborate joke for their benefit.

"It's true," I said soberly. "It's not a salary. I get a percentage of
every dollar that comes into the box office. Don't you
190 understand how it works?"

Obviously they did not, and I realized somewhat belatedly
that it had never occurred to either of them to translate good
fortune in the theater into anything more than what my
mother's friends defined as "making a good living." No wonder
195 my proposal had sounded lunatic, but now as the belief came
to them that what I had just said might be the literal truth, they
were suddenly seized with some of my own excitement. My
mother's reaction was a curious one. She burst into a peal of
laughter. She had a merry and ringing laugh and it was
200 contagious. My father and I joined in her laughter, though we
would have been hard put to tell exactly what we were
laughing at. I was reminded of that moment and of her
laughter long, long afterward, when I heard someone say,
"Nothing makes people laugh like money—the rich get wrinkles
205 from laughing." It was said sardonically, of course, but it is not

without an element of truth. Money does generate its own kind
of excitement, and its sudden acquisition creates an ambiance
of gaiety and merriment that would be nonsense to deny or not
210 to enjoy. It induces, moreover, a momentum of its own.
Everything moves with an unaccustomed and almost
miraculous speed.

We were all ready to leave in less than an hour, despite the
fact that there were more things of heaven and earth in that
215 box in the closet than could be contained in one suitcase. I
carried the box, my father and brother each carried a suitcase,
and my mother, her victory complete, hugged a brown paper
parcel of last-minute treasures that had turned up in an old tin
box. We walked out the door and waited in the lobby while my
220 brother hurried out in the rain to try to get a taxi. The rain was
pouring down in a great solid sheet now, and gusts of wind
were slashing it against the glass doors of the lobby and I was
seized by a sudden and irresistible impulse.

"I forgot something," I said shortly. "I'll be right back."
225 I unlocked the door of the empty apartment and closed and
locked it again carefully behind me. I took one quick look
around to keep the memory of that room forever verdant and
then walked to each window and threw it wide open. The rain
whipped in through the windows like a broadside of artillery
230 fire. I watched a large puddle form on the floor and spread
darkly over the carpet. The rain streamed across the top and
down the legs of the dining-room table and splashed over the
sideboard and the china closet. It soaked the armchair and
cascaded down the sofa. It peppered the wallpaper with large
235 wet blotches, and the wind sent two lamps crashing to the floor.
I kicked them out of my way and walked over to the daybed,
which was still dry, and pulled it out into the middle of the
room, where a fresh onset of wind and rain immediately
drenched it. I looked around me with satisfaction, feeling
240 neither guilty nor foolish. More reasonable gestures have
seldom succeeded in giving me half the pleasure this
meaningless one did. It was the hallmark, the final signature, of
defiance and liberation. Short of arson, I could do no more.

I slammed the door behind me without looking back.

VOCABULARY EXERCISE

In the blank space, write the word or phrase that best completes each sentence.

imperative (line 120)   patriotic (line 63)
drab and ugly (lines 36–38)   forbidding
                          and impenetrable (lines 27–28)

1. The grandeur of the New York City skyline seems

   _____ to him.

2. Moss feels proud to live in a country where this kind of success is

   possible; he feels _____.

3. Moss feels that it is _____ for him to make the

   theater his life's goal.

4. When Moss looks at the family apartment, he thinks it is

   _____.

COMPREHENSION EXERCISE

Put the following sentences in the order in which they happened in the story, by numbering them 1 to 4.

_____ **a.** Moss takes a cab ride from New York City home to Brooklyn.

_____ **b.** He tells his family that they are moving to a hotel immediately
          and can only pack one suitcase.

_____ **c.** He waits for newspaper reviews of the opening night of his
          play.

_____ **d.** When Moss goes back inside to say "goodbye" to the Brooklyn apartment where he has lived since childhood, he opens the window so that it will rain in on the furniture.

COMPREHENSION QUESTIONS

1. What kind of reviews does his play get?

2. When Moss Hart looks at the New York skyline from the taxi, it looks different. In what way? How does it make him feel?

3. Why does he feel patriotic during the taxi ride?

4. What problems does he have with the idea of being rich?

5. What kind of life did he and his family have before his success?

6. Why does he make the family move out of their apartment?

7. Why does he open the window and let it rain in on the furniture?

WRITING STRATEGY ACTIVITIES

1. Think of a transition word for each of the sentences that would link the sentence parts together logically. Write it in the blank.

   a. The dessert you made looks great, _____ I would like to have some.

   b. _____ the plane leaves, I would prefer to wait in the cafe.

   c. I would like to sit down _____ I have been on my feet all day.

   d. I have already eaten, _____ I will sit with you _____ you have your supper.

e. Did you have some popcorn _____ you watched the movie last night?

f. _____ I go to bed, I am going to fix myself some spice tea.

g. That pie smells good, _____ I have just eaten and am full.

h. _____ she is only 13, she looks much older.

i. _____ it rains, I have to bring the porch furniture in.

j. I slept _____ 9:00 this morning.

2. Look back over the excerpt from *Act One* and underline at least five transition words that clarify the relationship between different actions and events.

3. Go back to the prereading exercise you wrote regarding a change you would make if you suddenly became rich. Experiment with three different ways to write about that idea—to glue it together. For example, one paragraph could be laid out in a logical time order—what would you do first, second, third, etc? A second treatment of your idea could be in the form of a poem, and a third approach could be to simply write a loose stream of thoughts (like in the story "Girl" in Unit 1). Or you may find other creative ways to approach your idea.

TOPICS FOR DISCUSSION OR WRITING

1. At some time in your life, you have succeeded in doing something that you thought was difficult—if not impossible. It could be something that now seems not so important, like riding a bicycle; or it could be overcoming a major obstacle. Think about something that you have done that you were successful at. Describe your feelings before and after your success.

2. Ask two or three people about something that they have succeeded at in their life—something that they are proud of themselves for. Do any of their responses surprise you? If so, why? Report your "survey results" to the class.

SECTION 6

PREREADING

An obstacle is anything that impedes or gets in the way of something happening. Take a few minutes and list *anything* that comes to mind when you think of the word *obstacle*. Then share your associations with your classmates and see what associations you have in common.

The last selection in this unit is "Obstacle." As you read it, think about obstacles that keep you from getting where you want to go in your life.

OBSTACLE
Sally Jorgensen

Squat in the middle of the gameboard,
I can see the squares I've come from
And the best moves to make next.
I just can't see the square I'm on now
5 As well as when I leave it.

COMPREHENSION QUESTIONS

1. What does the title mean? What or who is the obstacle here?

2. Can you restate the meaning of the poem?

3. A gameboard here refers to a playing surface with paths or squares that you could move a "game piece" along, forward or backward, perhaps by a throw of dice. A chess board or checkerboard is one type of game board. What is the game board a metaphor for in the poem?

TOPICS FOR DISCUSSION OR WRITING

1. In the poem, the speaker can't understand what is happening to her while she is in the middle of an experience. *Before* or *after* the experience, she is better able to make sense of it and get it in perspective. Does an experience come to mind for you that you were caught up in, but could not fully grasp at the time? For example, have you had an experience that now seems stressful or painful, but you were not fully in touch with these feelings at the time? If so, write about it.

2. Are you your own worst obstacle? In what ways do you get in your own way? What characteristics keep you from acting the way you would like to or accomplishing some of the things you want to do? Write about these *internal* "obstacles" to success.

3. Write a letter to an advice columnist in the local newspaper (such as Dear Abby) about a problem you are having or an obstacle in your life. After you have done that, either answer your own letter or exchange your letter with a classmate and have him or her respond to your problem. (You could also choose to actually send your letter to a real advice columnist.)

UNIT 5 WORKING

People spend most of their lives working. The most gratifying work is that which uses and develops our talents well, meshes with our values, and furthers our life goals. Unfortunately, a lot of people dislike their jobs. However, there are also people who enjoy their work so much that it feels like play. They are particularly fortunate, as are those whose work is appreciated and rewarded by society.

If you work, do you enjoy it and feel appreciated? Is there someone whose line of work you envy? As you study this unit, think about your own work experiences—both inside and outside of the home. What aspects of those experiences have been most gratifying and what aspects have been most stressful or difficult?

SECTION 1

PREREADING

If you were looking for someone to work with, what qualities would you look for? Make a list of five different qualities of a good worker. Compare your list with a classmate's. Are there characteristics that you agree with? Disagree with?

In the following poem by Marge Piercy, "To Be of Use," the speaker believes that it is not so important *what* you do, as *how well* you do it. Do you agree?

TO BE OF USE
Marge Piercy

The people I love the best
jump into work head first
without dallying in the shadows
and swim off with sure strokes almost out of sight.
5   They seem to become natives of that element,
the black sleek heads of seals
bouncing like half-submerged balls.

I love people who harness themselves, an ox to a
    heavy cart,
10 who pull like water buffalo, with massive patience,
who strain in the mud and the muck to move things
    forward,
who do what has to be done, again and again.

I want to be with people who submerge
15 in the task, who go into the fields to harvest
and work in a row and pass the bags along,
who stand in the line and haul in their places,
who are not parlor generals and field deserters
but move in a common rhythm
20 when the food must come in or the fire be put out.

The work of the world is common as mud.
Botched, it smears the hands, crumbles to dust.
But the thing worth doing well done
has a shape that satisfies, clean and evident.
25 Greek amphoras for wine and oil,
Hopi vases that held corn, are put in museums
but you know they were made to be used.
The pitcher cries for water to carry
and a person for work that is real.

"To Be of Use" is reprinted from CIRCLES ON THE WATER by Marge Piercy. Copyright © 1973 by Marge Piercy. Reprinted by permission of Alfred A. Knopf, Inc.

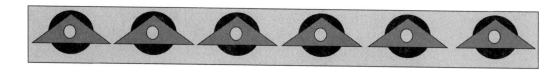

VOCABULARY EXERCISE

Match the words below with their definitions.

a. dallying   (line 03)
b. submerged (line 07)
c. harness   (line 08)
d. massive   (line 10)

e. parlor   (line 18)
f. deserter   (line 18)
g. botched   (line 22)
h. patience (line 10)

_____ huge in size or amount

_____ the ability to handle
    problems calmly,
    carefully, and
    without complaining

_____ messed up

_____ under the surface

_____ wasting time

_____ to attach an animal to
    a wagon or cart

_____ a person who
    abandons his or her
    responsibilities

_____ old-fashioned sitting
    room

Using words from the list in the previous exercise, complete the sentences so that they make sense.

1. The woman _____ the job of wallpapering

   my bathroom.

2. She had no _____ with detailed work like

   that.

3. I often saw her _____ when she should have

   been working.

4. She needed someone to " _____ " her to the task.

5. In the end she was a _____ because she

never actually finished the wallpapering job.

6. The whole mess gave me a _____ headache!

COMPREHENSION QUESTIONS

1. How is a pitcher used as a metaphor for people?

2. How does this comparison explain the title of the poem?

3. Circle some of the other comparisons in the poem that are used to describe workers and types of work. Which of these comparisons are metaphors, and which are similes and why?

4. Sum up in your own words the kind of worker that the speaker admires.

5. From what point of view is the poem written—first person, third person, or from an omniscient (all-knowing) perspective?

TOPICS FOR DISCUSSION OR WRITING

1. Would you describe yourself as the type of worker that the speaker admires? If not, how are you different? Describe what kind of employee you are, what your work habits are, and what kind of working conditions you prefer.

2. Would any of your supervisors or co-workers (or teachers or classmates) describe you differently than the way you described yourself in the previous question? If so, how?

3. Describe your ideal job or work situation. (If your answer is "not to have to work at all," describe how you would then spend your time!)

4. Distinctions are often made between work and play. What is the difference between them? Do you think these distinctions are valid or are work and play sometimes the same? Do you think that children make those distinctions? Why or why not?

SECTION 2

PREREADING

Write for a few minutes about your first day at a job or at school. What did you feel? What were your concerns? You may want to share your ideas with a classmate, your teacher, or the whole class. If you prefer, write your answers in a private journal.

The next story by Sandra Cisneros, "The First Job," from her book, *The House on Mango Street*, is about a young woman's experiences in her first job. As you read the story, think about your first day on a new job and how you felt. Would you react as she does?

THE FIRST JOB
Sandra Cisneros

It wasn't as if I didn't want to work. I did. I had even gone to the social security office the month before to get my social security number. I needed money. The Catholic high school cost a lot, and Papa said nobody went to public school unless you
5 wanted to turn out bad.

I thought I'd find an easy job, the kind other kids had, working in the dime store or maybe a hotdog stand. And though I hadn't started looking yet, I thought I might the week after next. But when I came home that afternoon, all wet
10 because Tito had pushed me into the open water hydrant—only I had sort of let him—Mama called me in the kitchen before I could even go and change, and Aunt Lala was sitting there drinking her coffee with a spoon. Aunt Lala said she had found

a job for me at Peter Pan Photo Finishers on North Broadway
15 where she worked and told me I was to show up tomorrow
saying I was one year older and that was that.

So the next morning I put on the navy blue dress that made
me look older and borrowed money for lunch and bus fare
because Aunt Lala said I wouldn't get paid 'til the next Friday
20 and I went in and saw the boss of the Peter Pan Photo Finishers
on North Broadway where Aunt Lala worked and lied about
my age like she told me to and sure enough I started that same
day.

In my job I had to wear white gloves. I was supposed to
25 match negatives with their prints, just look at the picture and
look for the same one on the negative strip, put it in the
envelope, and do the next one. That's all. I didn't know where
the envelopes were coming from or where they were going. I
just did what I was told.
30 It was real easy and I guess I wouldn't have minded it except
that you got tired after a while and I didn't know if I could sit
down or not, and then I started sitting down only when the two
ladies next to me did. After a while they started to laugh and
came up to me and said I could sit when I wanted to and I said
35 I knew.

When lunch time came I was scared to eat alone in the
company lunchroom with all those men and ladies looking, so I
ate real fast standing in one of the washroom stalls and had lots
of time left over so I went back to work early. But then break
40 time came and not knowing where else to go I went into the
coatroom because there was a bench there.

I guess it was the time for the night shift or middle shift to
arrive because a few older people came in and punched the
time clock and an older Oriental man said hello and we talked
45 for a while about my just starting and he said we could be
friends and next time to go in the lunchroom and sit with him
and I felt better. He had nice eyes and I didn't feel so nervous
anymore. Then he asked if I knew what day it was and when I
said I didn't he said it was his birthday and would I please give
50 him a birthday kiss. I thought I would because he was so old
and just as I was about to put my lips on his cheek, he grabs
my face with both hands and kisses me hard on the mouth and
doesn't let go.

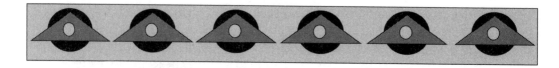

COMPREHENSION EXERCISE

Complete the sentence with a logical word or phrase. (Try each of them without going back to the story, then check your answers.)

1. In order to work in the United States, everyone needs to have a

   _____ number.

2. The speaker in the story gets a job at a _____

   _____ store.

3. She is supposed to match _____ with their _____

   _____ .

4. She has to wear white _____ when she handles

   these materials.

5. She eats lunch by herself standing up in the _____

   _____, and later during her break she goes into the

   _____ because there is a bench where

   she can sit down.

6. At first _____ is nice to her and invites her to sit at

   his table in the lunchroom.

COMPREHENSION QUESTIONS

1. How does the narrator in the story get the job?

2. What kind of work does she do?

3. What are some of the things she does that illustrate that she is nervous on her first day?

4. Describe her encounter with the older Oriental man.

TOPICS FOR DISCUSSION OR WRITING

1. In order to qualify for the job the narrator lied about her age. Do you think she should or should not have done this? Where do your fellow classmates stand on this question?
2. Why do you think that the man kisses her? Is he just being friendly or do you think he takes advantage of her?
3. How do you think she should react to his kissing her? Continue the story where it leaves off, and describe what you think might have happened next. Maintain the narrator's conversational tone, as though you are still confiding in a close friend.
4. Write about an experience that you (or someone else) may have had where the person is taken advantage of in a situation because he or she is new or unfamiliar with the "rules." (It does not have to be an unwanted sexual encounter—legally referred to as *sexual harassment*, but it can be any situation where someone's innocence or ignorance was taken advantage of.)
5. Take your writing in topics 2 or 3 and turn either situation into a dialogue between two people. How would the person who is being taken advantage of handle the situation? What does he or she say and do? Act out these roles with a classmate.

WRITING STRATEGY LESSON: TONE OF VOICE

Writers adapt the style of language used to the tone of voice of the narrator or the characters they are writing about. Just as people have different speech patterns and assume different tones of voice to communicate particular messages, writers try to capture these various aspects of language usage in their writing. The tone of voice of a story or poem can be

▼ serious *or* humorous (such as with a heavy versus a light tone),

▼ formal *or* informal,

▼ conversational or colloquial—as though the speaker is talking casually with the reader using familiar language, or

▼ a loose stream of thoughts (interior monologue).

Think back over some of the stories and poems you have read in earlier units. Do readings come to mind that are examples of the styles just mentioned? Because a theme throughout the book is the *personal voice*, most of the writings are informal and conversational, rather than formal. And although many of the writings have a serious message, humorous comments are sometimes interwoven throughout the story. Probably the loosest style of writing thus far is "Girl" by Jamaica Kincaid from Unit 1. It is essentially an interior monologue; the speaker is not addressing her thoughts to the outside world in a typical story or essay form.

What is the point of view of "The First Job"? How would you describe the writing style and the tone of voice that comes across? Serious or light? Formal or informal? Conversational? The story makes some serious points despite the light style of the writing. Would you agree that it is conversational in tone? The narrator confides in you, the reader, about her first day of work as though you are her best friend. Look back at the story and find three or four specific examples of this conversational writing style.

SECTION 3

PREREADING

Imagine that you have applied for a job and the interviewer tells you directly or implies that you cannot have the job because you are too young or too old, the wrong sex, or the wrong color. Choose one of these situations and write whatever comes to mind about how you might feel and react in such a situation. You may want to share your ideas with a classmate, your teacher, or the whole class. If you prefer, write your answers in a private journal.

The next story is also about getting a job, and it takes place in the 1940s during World War II. The story is an excerpt from Maya Angelou's autobiography, *I Know Why the Caged Bird Sings*. It is an inspirational story about one person's battle against discrimination. As you read it, think about whether you would have had the "gumption" to persevere the way Maya did. Or would you have reacted differently?

I KNOW WHY THE CAGED BIRD SINGS
Excerpt
Maya Angelou

My room had all the cheeriness of a dungeon and the appeal of a tomb. It was going to be impossible to stay there, but leaving held no attraction for me, either. The answer came to me with the suddenness of a collision. I would go to work.

5 Mother wouldn't be difficult to convince; after all, in school I was a year ahead of my grade and Mother was a firm believer in self-sufficiency. In fact, she'd be pleased to think that I had that much gumption, that much of her in my character. (She liked to speak of herself as the original "do-it-yourself" girl.)

10 Once I had settled on getting a job, all that remained was to decide which kind of job I was most fitted for. My intellectual pride had kept me from selecting typing, shorthand or filing as subjects in school, so office work was ruled out. War plants and shipyards demanded birth certificates, and mine would reveal

15 me to be fifteen, and ineligible for work. So the well-paying defense jobs were also out. Women had replaced men on the streetcars as conductors and motormen, and the thought of sailing up and down the hills of San Francisco in a dark-blue uniform, with a money changer at my belt, caught my fancy.

20 Mother was as easy as I had anticipated. The world was moving so fast, so much money was being made, so many people were dying in Guam, and Germany, that hordes of strangers became good friends overnight. How could she have the time to think about my academic career?

25 To her question of what I planned to do, I replied that I would get a job on the streetcars. She rejected the proposal with, "They don't accept black people on the streetcars."

I would like to claim an immediate fury that was followed by the noble determination to break the restricting tradition. But

30 the truth is, my first reaction was one of disappointment. I'd pictured myself, dressed in a neat blue serge suit, my money changer swinging jauntily at my waist, and a cheery smile for the passengers that would make their own work day brighter.

From disappointment, I gradually ascended the emotional

35 ladder to haughty indignation, and finally to that state of stubbornness where the mind is locked like the jaws of an enraged bulldog.

I would go to work on the streetcars and wear a blue serge suit. Mother gave me her support with one of her usual terse asides, "That's what you want to do? Then nothing beats a trial but a failure. Give it everything you've got. I've told you many times, 'Can't Do is like Don't Care.' Neither of them has a home."

Translated, that meant there is nothing a person can't do, and there should be nothing a human being doesn't care about. It was the most positive encouragement I could have hoped for.

In the offices of the Market Street Railway Company, the receptionist seemed as surprised to see me there as I was surprised to find the interior dingy and drab. Somehow I had expected waxed surfaces and carpeted floors. If I had met no resistance, I might have decided against working for such a poor-mouth-looking concern. As it was, I explained that I had come to see about a job. She asked, was I sent by an agency, and when I replied that I was not, she told me they were only accepting applicants from agencies.

The classified pages of the morning papers had listed advertisements for motorettes and conductorettes, and I reminded her of that. She gave me a face full of astonishment that my suspicious nature would not accept.

60 "I am applying for the job listed in this morning's *Chronicle*, and I'd like to be presented to your personnel manager." While I spoke in supercilious accents, and looked at the room as if I had an oil well in my own backyard, my armpits were being pricked by millions of hot pointed needles. She saw her escape
65 and dived into it.

"He's out. He's out for the day. You might call him tomorrow, and if he's in, I'm sure you can see him." Then she swiveled her chair around on its rusty screws, and with that I was supposed to be dismissed.

70 "May I ask his name?"
She half turned, acting surprised to find me still there.
"His name? Whose name?"
"Your personnel manager."
We were firmly joined in the hypocrisy to play out the scene.

75 "The personnel manager? Oh, he's Mr. Cooper, but I'm not sure you'll find him here tomorrow. He's . . . Oh, but you can try."
"Thank you."
"You're welcome."

80 And I was out of the musty room and into the even mustier lobby. In the street I saw the receptionist and myself going faithfully through paces that were stale with familiarity, although I had never encountered that kind of situation before and, probably, neither had she. We were like actors who,
85 knowing the play by heart, were still able to cry afresh over the old tragedies and laugh spontaneously at the comic situations.

The miserable little encounter had nothing to do with me, the me of me, any more that it had to do with that silly clerk. The incident was a recurring dream concocted years before by
90 whites, and it eternally came back to haunt us all. The secretary and I were like people in a scene where, because of harm done by one ancestor to another, we were bound to duel to the death. Also, because the play must end somewhere.

I went further than forgiving the clerk; I accepted her as a
95 fellow victim of the same puppeteer.

On the streetcar, I put my fare into the box, and the conductorette looked at me with the usual hard eyes of white contempt. "Move into the car, please move on in the car." She patted her money changer.

100   Her Southern nasal accent sliced my meditation, and I looked deep into my thoughts. All lies, all comfortable lies. The receptionist was not innocent and neither was I. The whole charade we had played out in that waiting room had directly to do with me, black, and her, white.

105   I wouldn't move into the streetcar but stood on the ledge over the conductor, glaring. My mind shouted so energetically that the announcement made my veins stand out, and my mouth tighten into a prune.

    I WOULD HAVE THE JOB. I WOULD BE A CONDUCTORETTE
110 AND SLING A FULL MONEY CHANGER FROM MY BELT. I WOULD.

    The next three weeks were a honeycomb of determination with apertures for the days to go in and out. The black organizations to whom I appealed for support bounced me
115 back and forth like a shuttlecock on a badminton court. Why did I insist on that particular job? Openings were going begging that paid nearly twice the money. The minor officials with whom I was able to win an audience thought me mad. Possibly I was.

120   Downtown San Francisco became alien and cold, and the streets I had loved in a personal familiarity were unknown lanes that twisted with malicious intent. My trips to the streetcar office were of the frequency of a person on salary. The struggle expanded. I was no longer in conflict only with the Market
125 Street Railway but with the marble lobby of the building that housed its offices, and elevators and their operators.

    During this period of strain, Mother and I began our first steps on the long path toward mutual adult admiration. She never asked for reports and I didn't offer any details. But every
130 morning she made breakfast, gave me carfare and lunch money, as if I were going to work. She comprehended that in the struggle lies the joy. That I was no glory seeker was obvious to her, and that I had to exhaust every possibility before giving in was also clear.

135   On my way out of the house one morning she said, "Life is going to give you just what you put in it. Put your whole heart in everything you do, and pray; then you can wait." Another time she reminded me that, "God helps those who help themselves." She had a store of aphorisms that she dished out as

140 the occasion demanded. Strangely, as bored as I was with her clichés, her inflection gave them something new, and set me thinking for a little while at least. Later, when asked how I got my job, I was never able to say exactly. I only knew that one day, which was tiresomely like all the others before it, I sat in

145 the Railway office, waiting to be interviewed. The receptionist called me to her desk and shuffled a bundle of papers to me. They were job application forms. She said they had to be filled in triplicate. I had little time to wonder if I had won or not, for the standard questions reminded me of the necessity for lying.

150 How old was I? List my previous jobs, starting from the last held and go backward to the first. How much money did I earn, and why did I leave the position? Give two references (not relatives). I kept my face blank (an old art) and wrote quickly the fable of Marguerite Johnson, aged nineteen, former companion and

155 driver for Mrs. Annie Henderson (a White Lady) in Stamps, Arkansas.

I was given blood tests, aptitude tests, and physical coordination tests; then, on a blissful day, I was hired as the first black on the San Francisco streetcars.

160 Mother gave me the money to have my blue serge suit tailored, and I learned to fill out work cards, operate the money changer and punch transfers. The time crowded together, and at an End of Days I was swinging on the back of the rackety

165   trolley, smiling sweetly and persuading my charges to "step
forward in the car, please."
     For one whole semester the streetcars and I shimmied up and
scooted down the sheer hills of San Francisco. I lost some of my
need for the black ghetto's shielding-sponge quality, as I
170   clanged and cleared my way down Market Street, with its
honky-tonk homes for homeless sailors, past the quiet retreat of
Golden Gate Park, and along closed undwelled-in-looking
dwellings of the Sunset District.
     My workshifts were split so haphazardly that it was easy to
175   believe that my superiors had chosen them maliciously. Upon
mentioning my suspicions to Mother, she said, "Don't you worry
about it. You ask for what you want, and you pay for what you
get. And I'm going to show you that it ain't no trouble when you
pack double."
180   She stayed awake to drive me out to the car barn at four-
thirty in the mornings, or to pick me up when I was relieved just
before dawn. Her awareness of life's perils convinced her that
while I would be safe on the public conveyances, she "wasn't
about to trust a taxi driver with her baby."
185   When the spring classes began, I resumed my commitment
with formal education. I was so much wiser and older, so much
more independent, with a bank account and clothes that I had
bought for myself, that I was sure I had learned and earned the
magic formula that would make me a part of the life my
190   contemporaries led.
     Not a bit of it. Within weeks, I realized that my schoolmates
and I were on paths moving away from each other. They were
concerned and excited over the approaching football games.
They concentrated great interest on who was worthy of being
195   student body president, and when the metal bands would be
removed from their teeth, while I remembered conducting a
streetcar in the uneven hours of the morning.

VOCABULARY EXERCISE

Fill in the blanks in the sentences with a word from the list that makes sense. You may have to change the form of the word to fit the particular sentence.

victim	(line 95)	inflection	(line 141)
ineligibility	(line 15)	anticipated	(line 20)
proud	(line 12)	determination	(line 29)
malicious	(line 122)	convince	(line 05)
contempt	(line 98)	aptitude	(line 162)

1. Maya tries to _____ the receptionist to let her

   see the personnel manager.

2. Maya does not _____ the response she gets

   from the receptionist.

3. She feels that she and the receptionist are both

   _____ of the racist society they live in.

4. Maya's _____ and _____

   make her persevere in the battle until she finally gets the job as

   streetcar conductor.

5. Maya is accustomed to seeing _____ in the

   eyes of white people when they look at her. She can also hear it in

   the _____ in their voices.

6. Although she has to lie about her age in order to be

_____ for the job, she has a special

_____ for the work.

7. Although Maya resents the prejudice she encounters, she is not

_____ in return toward whites.

COMPREHENSION EXERCISES

Complete the following sentences with the correct information from the story. Try to do the exercise without looking back at the story. Then check your answers.

1. Maya describes her room at the beginning of the story as

_____

_____.

2. One of the reasons that Maya wants to be a streetcar conductor is

that she likes _____

_____.

3. She feels that she and the receptionist are both _____

_____ of the racist society they live in.

_____.

4. Maya finally gets the job as a streetcar conductor because of her

_____.

5. Compared to her classmates at school, Maya seems _____

_____.

COMPREHENSION QUESTIONS

1. The story takes place during the Second World War. How does this affect Maya's chances of getting the job she wants?

2. Maya's mother tells her that they do not accept black people for work on the streetcars. How does she react? How do her feelings change?

3. Maya and her mother admire each other. Why? Support your response with specific references from the story.

4. When Maya goes back to school, how is she different as a result of the job? How does it change her relationships with her school friends?

5. Maya says that the encounter with the receptionist "had nothing to do with me, with the me of me, any more than it had to do with that silly clerk." She says that the receptionist is a "fellow victim of the same puppeteer." What does she mean by these comments?

TOPICS FOR DISCUSSION OR WRITING

1. How would you have dealt with the discrimination and rejection that Maya encountered? Would you have persevered the way that she did, or would you have responded differently?

2. Now put yourself in the place of the receptionist. Do you think that she is aware of the system of discrimination that she is perpetuating? Do you think she feels any conflict? Would you act differently toward Maya if you were the receptionist?

3. Look back at the prereading exercise you did before you read the story. Draft a letter to the interviewer in that hypothetical (invented) situation responding to his or her—or the company's—discriminatory position. Share your letters with classmates and see if the class can arrive at one or two "best" ways to handle this type of experience, which in fact is illegal in most job-hiring situations in the United States.

4. Have you ever encountered discrimination in a job situation because of race, gender, or cultural differences? How did it make you feel, and how did you handle the situation?

5. What is the most difficult obstacle or task that you have run into in a job situation? How did you deal with it? After everyone in the class has had a chance to think about this question, interview a classmate and report back to the class.

WRITING STRATEGY ACTIVITIES

Although Maya Angelou's story is about a very painful and serious experience, her writing style contains a great deal of irony and wit. *Irony* is an unexpected juxtaposition of two situations. An author employs irony to shift the reader's normal perspective of a particular situation. There is irony, for example, in Angelou's showing us that the receptionist is as much a victim of a discriminatory society as is Maya. At a superficial level, we might have considered Maya to be the only victim in the story. The idea that they are both victims introduces a much more complex and provocative perspective for the reader to contemplate.

The author uses numerous writing strategies (sometimes referred to as *literary devices*) to reveal the voice and perspective of the narrator. She is especially witty and adept in her use of metaphor and hyperbole. Hyperbole (pronounced HI-PER'-BU-LEE) is deliberate exaggeration or the use of an extreme reference to make a point. The author's metaphors and similes are often hyperboles, such as in the description of her room (lines 1–2) as having "all the cheeriness of a dungeon and the appeal of a tomb." Maya's sense of humor and unique perspective about her situation come across through her language.

Can you find other examples of irony, wit, metaphor, and hyperbole in the story? Circle at least five lines that you find witty in the story and decide if they are examples of any of these writing strategies.

SECTION 4

PREREADING

In your journal, write about a person that you admire who is not educated. Explain why you admire this person. You may want to share your ideas with a classmate, your teacher, or the whole class.

The next story, "Señor Payroll," by William Barrett takes place in the Southwest where there are many new immigrants from Mexico. Many of these people have had little or no schooling. The workers in this story may not be well educated, but they are very clever. As you read the story, think about how you would have dealt with the situation if you were the narrator.

SEÑOR PAYROLL
William Barrett

Larry and I were Junior Engineers in the gas plant, which means that we were clerks. Anything that could be classified as paper work came to the flat double desk across which we faced each other. The Main Office downtown sent us a bewildering
5 array of orders and rules that were to be put into effect.

Junior Engineers were beneath the notice of everyone except the Mexican laborers at the plant. To them we were the visible form of a distant, unknowable paymaster. We were Señor Payroll.
10 Those Mexicans were great workmen: the aristocrats among them were the stokers, big men who worked Herculean eight-

hour shifts in the fierce heat of the retorts. They scooped coal with huge shovels and hurled it with uncanny aim at tiny doors. The coal streamed out from the shovels like black water
15 from a high-pressure nozzle, and never missed the narrow opening. The stokers worked stripped to the waist, and there was pride and dignity in them. Few men could do such work, and they were the few.

The Company paid its men only twice a month, on the fifth
20 and on the twentieth. To a Mexican, this was absurd. What man with money will make it last fifteen days? If he hoarded money beyond the spending of three days, he was a miser — and when, Señor, did the blood of Spain flow in the veins of misers? Hence, it was the custom for our stokers to appear every
25 third or fourth day to draw the money due them.

There was a certain elasticity in the Company rules, and Larry and I sent the necessary forms to the Main Office and received an "advance" against a man's pay check. Then, one day, Downtown favored us with a memorandum.
30 "There have been too many abuses of the advance-against-wages privilege. Hereafter, no advance against wages will be made to any employee except in a case of genuine emergency."

We had no sooner posted the notice when in came stoker
35 Juan Garcia. He asked for an advance. I pointed to the notice.
He spelled it through slowly, and then said, "What does this
mean, this 'genuine emergency'?"

I explained to him patiently that the Company was kind and
sympathetic, but that it was a great nuisance to have to pay
40 wages every few days. If someone was ill or if money was
urgently needed for some other good reason, then the
Company would make an exception to the rule.

Juan Garcia turned his hat over and over slowly in his big
hands. "I do not get my money?"
45 "Next payday, Juan. On the twentieth."

He went out silently and I felt a little ashamed of myself. I
looked across the desk at Larry. He avoided my eyes.

In the next hour two other stokers came in, looked at the
notice, had it explained and walked solemnly out; then no
50 more came. What we did not know was that Juan Garcia, Pete
Mendoza, and Francisco Gonzalez had spread the word, and
that every Mexican in the plant was explaining the order to
every other Mexican. "To get money now, the wife must be sick.
There must be medicine for the baby."
55 The next morning Juan Garcia's wife was practically dying,
Pete Mendoza's mother would hardly last the day, there was a
veritable epidemic among children, and, just for variety, there
was one sick father. We always suspected that the old man was
really sick; no Mexican would otherwise have thought of him.
60 At any rate, nobody paid Larry and me to examine private
lives; we made out our forms with an added line describing the
"genuine emergency." Our people got paid.

That went on for a week. Then came a new order, curt and to
the point: "Hereafter, employees will be paid ONLY on the fifth
65 and the twentieth of the month. No exceptions will be made
except in the cases of employees leaving the service of the
Company."

The notice went up on the board, and we explained its
significance gravely. "No Juan Garcia, we cannot advance
70 your wages. It is too bad about your wife and your cousins and
your aunts, but there is a new rule."

Juan Garcia went out and thought it over. He thought out
loud with Mendoza and Gonzalez and Ayala, then, in the
morning, he was back, "I am quitting this company for a
75 different job. You pay me now?"

We argued that it was a good company and that it loved its employees like children, but in the end we paid off, because Juan Garcia quit. And so did Gonzalez, Mendoza, Obregon, Ayala and Ortez, the best stokers, men who could not be
80 replaced.

Larry and I looked at each other; we knew what was coming in about three days. One of our duties was to sit on the hiring line early each morning, engaging transient workers for the handy gangs. Any man was accepted who could walk up and
85 ask for a job without falling down. Never before had we been called upon to hire such skilled virtuosos as stokers for handy-gang work, but we were called upon to hire them now.

The day foreman was wringing his hands and asking the Almighty if he was personally supposed to shovel this
90 condemned coal, while there in a stolid, patient line were skilled men—Garcia, Mendoza, and others—waiting to be hired. We hired them, of course. There was nothing else to do.

Every day we had a line of resigning stokers and another line of stokers seeking work. Our paper work became very
95 complicated. At the Main Office they were jumping up and down. The procession of forms showing Juan Garcia's resigning and being hired over and over again was too much for them. Sometimes Downtown had Garcia on the payroll twice at the same time when someone down there was slow in entering a
100 resignation. Our phone rang early and often.

Tolerantly and patiently we explained: "There's nothing we can do if a man wants to quit, and if there are stokers available when the plant needs stokers, we hire them."

Out of chaos, Downtown issued another order. I read it and
105 whistled. Larry looked at it and said, "It is going to be very quiet around here."

The order read: "Hereafter, no employee who resigns may be rehired within a period of 30 days."

Juan Garcia was due for another resignation, and when he
110 came in we showed him the order and explained that standing in line the next day would do him no good if he resigned today. "Thirty days is a long time, Juan."

It was a grave matter and he took time to reflect on it. So did Gonzalez, Mendoza, Ayala and Ortez. Ultimately, however, they
115 were all back — and all resigned.

We did our best to dissuade them and we were sad about the parting. This time it was for keeps and they shook hands with us

solemnly. It was very nice knowing us. Larry and I looked at each other when they were gone and we both knew that
120 neither of us had been pulling for Downtown to win this duel. It was a blue day.

In the morning, however, they were all back in line. With the utmost gravity, Juan Garcia informed me that he was a stoker looking for a job.
125 "No dice, Juan" I said. "Come back in thirty days. I warned you."

His eyes looked straight into mine without a flicker. "There is some mistake, Señor," he said. "I am Manuel Hernandez. I work as the stoker in Pueblo, in Santa Fe, in many places."
130 I stared at him, remembering the sick wife and the babies without medicine, the mother-in-law in the hospital, the many resignations and the rehirings. I knew that there was a gas plant in Pueblo, and that there wasn't any in Santa Fe; but who was I to argue with a man about his own name? A stoker is a
135 stoker.

So I hired him. I hired Gonzalez, too, who swore that his name was Carrera, and Ayala, who had shamelessly become Smith.

Three days later the resigning started.

Within a week our payroll read like a history of Latin
140 America. Everyone was on it: Lopez and Obregon, Villa, Diaz, Batista, Gomez, and even San Martin and Bolivar. Finally Larry and I weary of staring at familiar faces and writing unfamiliar names, went to the Superintendent and told him the whole story. He tried not to grin, and said, "Damned nonsense!"
145 The next day the orders were taken down. We called our most prominent stokers into the office and pointed to the board. No rules any more.

"The next time we hire you hombres," Larry said grimly, "come in under the names you like best, because that's the way
150 you are going to stay on the books."

They looked at us and they looked at the board: then for first time in the long duel, their teeth flashed white. "Si Señores," they said.

And so it was.

"Señor Payroll" by William Barrett. Copyright © 1943 by University Press in Dallas. Reprinted by permission of Harold Ober Associates, Inc.

VOCABULARY EXERCISE

Change the form of the vocabulary words at the left in order that each is grammatically correct in the sentence that follows it.

visible

(line 07)

1. The payroll clerks, Larry and the narrator of the story, have greater _____ for the Mexican workers than do the company managers.

absurd

(line 20)

2. The payroll problems become _____ complicated after a while.

abuses

(line 30)

3. The company believes that the workers are _____ the privilege of pay advances.

sympathetic

(line 39)

4. Larry and the narrator _____ with the Mexican workers.

urgently

(line 41)

5. The workers feel an _____ need to get paid weekly.

significance

(line 69)

6. Each new rule _____ a change in company policy.

argued

(line 76)

7. For the workers, telling lies that follow the rules is easier than _____ with management.

VOCABULARY PRACTICE

Fill in the blanks with a word from the list that makes sense in the sentence.

exceptions	(line 65)	privilege	(line 31)
nuisance	(line 39)	emergency	(line 33)
misers	(line 24)	memorandum (memo)	(line 29)

1. People who are stingy and hoard their money are

   _____.

2. The management wants there to be no _____

   to the rule that workers are paid on the fifth and the twentieth of

   the month.

3. The workers deliberately make a _____ of

   themselves in order to get the advance.

4. The management feels that there are too many abuses of the

   advance pay _____.

5. Every time the management makes a new rule, they send a

   _____ to the payroll office.

6. When a "genuine _____" becomes the only

   reason why workers can be paid in advance, suddenly all of the

   workers have an illness or death in the family.

COMPREHENSION EXERCISE

Number the following sentences 1 to 8 in the order in which they occur in the story.

_____ The workers resign their jobs in order to get a paycheck, then get rehired.

_____ Management rules that the only exceptions to the payroll schedule are workers who are leaving the company.

_____ The management finally drops all of the rules and agrees to pay the workers when they need money.

_____ The payroll office frequently sends in forms in order that the workers can get an "advance" on their wages, rather than wait for a paycheck every two weeks.

_____ The workers change their names so that they can be rehired immediately after resigning.

_____ Management rules that no one can be rehired for 30 days after their resignation.

_____ The workers come to the office for pay advances because of family emergencies.

_____ A rule comes down from the main office that workers can get an advance only if it is a genuine emergency.

COMPREHENSION QUESTIONS

1. What does the title of the story mean?

2. What kind of work do the Mexican workers do?

3. Explain the problem about paydays.

4. How do the workers outsmart the management?

5. The narrator says, "Nobody paid Larry and me to examine private lives." What does he mean by this?

6. What does the narrator think about the lies that the workers tell? What evidence can you find in the story that reveals his attitude?

WRITING STRATEGY ACTIVITIES

One of the reasons that the story "Señor Payroll" is enjoyable to read is the narrator's wit in recounting the payroll saga. The style of humor could be called *tongue-in-cheek*. This is an idiom which means that the words come across as serious and straightforward, but are in fact humorous and ironic. (The origin of this idiom is probably that the tongue is being held in the cheek to keep from laughing and giving away the real intent of the comment.) Some examples of tongue-in-cheek humor in the story are as follows:

Example 1: "If he [the Mexican worker] hoarded money beyond the spending of three days, he was a miser—and when, Señor, did the blood of Spain flow in the veins of misers?" (lines 21–24)

> In what way is the author gently teasing about Latin personality traits here?

_____

_____

Example 2: "The next morning Juan Garcia's wife was practically dying, Pete Mendoza's mother would hardly last the day, there was a veritable epidemic among children, and, just for variety, there was one sick father." (lines 55–58)

> Although the sentences are written in a completely serious and straightforward manner, the passage is actually rather humorous. Are all of these people really ill as the words indicate?

_____

_____

Can you find other examples of tongue-in-cheek humor in the story? (Write them here and note the line numbers.)

_____

_____

TOPICS FOR DISCUSSION OR WRITING

1. Do you think that the speaker in the poem "To Be of Use" would admire the Mexican workers? Why or why not?

2. Although Larry and the narrator follow the rules of the company, they are sympathetic with the Mexican workers. If you were in their position, would you have felt any conflict between complying with company policies and supporting the workers? (Remember that the workers' clever "defiance" of the rules created a great deal of extra paperwork for the payroll clerks.) Would you have felt or acted differently than they did? Would your answer be the same if the management had threatened to fire you for supporting the Mexicans?

3. Have you ever experienced a conflict in a job situation between having to represent the management's values or policies on the one hand and wanting to support the needs of another group, such as the employees or customers? For example, have you ever been involved in a union disagreement between the management and the workers? If so, describe the situation and your feelings about it, as well as how you dealt with the conflict.

4. In "Señor Payroll," as well as in the excerpt from _I Know Why the Caged Bird Sings_, we pull for the "underdog"—for individuals who are losing, or expected to lose, in a struggle. Underdogs can be disadvantaged because of injustice or discrimination. Maya deals with an unfair—and now illegal—system in the United States, and the Mexican workers are unhappy about certain work policies that they find hard to live with. Compare and contrast the two different ways that each of these "underdogs" (Maya and the Mexicans) deal with their situations and are victorious in their struggle against larger, impersonal institutions.